The Minister
as
Shepherd

The Minister

as

Shepherd

by

Charles Jefferson

CLC ❖ PUBLICATIONS
Fort Washington, Pennsylvania 19034

Published by CLC ❖ Publications

U.S.A.
P.O. Box 1449, Fort Washington, PA 19034

GREAT BRITAIN
51 The Dean, Alresford, Hants. SO24 9BJ

AUSTRALIA
P.O. Box 419M, Manunda, QLD 4879

NEW ZEALAND
10 MacArthur Street, Feilding

This American edition revised and reset 1998

ISBN 0-87508-706-X

Copyright © 1998
CLC Ministries International
Fort Washington, PA

Scripture quotations are largely from the
American Standard Version (1901) of the Bible,
though the author at times paraphrases.

This printing 2001

Contents

Introduction

This book is one of perhaps a dozen in my library that I try to read again each year. It does my heart good! It reminds me of my privileges and responsibilities as one of God's shepherds, and it makes me want to do a better job of preaching the Word and pastoring my flock. And it always convicts me!

Charles E. Jefferson was no armchair preacher. For nearly forty years he pastored the influential Broadway Tabernacle in New York City. Combining effective preaching with consistent pastoral work, Dr. Jefferson built a strong testimony in a difficult place. When he died in 1937, he left behind more than a dozen helpful books that he had written; but perhaps the most helpful is the one you now hold in your hand.

We are being told these days that the church is dying, that we must get a "new look" or a "new message" or we will disappear completely. Without closing his eyes to the changes around him, Jefferson goes straight to the Bible for the answer: *let the preacher be a pastor and the flock will strengthen itself and increase.* No gimmicks, nothing spectacular: simply a dedicated man of God going in and out among his people with the refreshing Word of life.

These lectures were delivered in 1912, but there is a freshness and relevance about them because they are based on the unchanging Word of God. Human nature has not changed! Now as then, our cities are teeming with people who are as "sheep not having a shepherd." The growing isolation and loneliness of modern society presents a great opportunity for the pastor who has a shepherd's heart.

May the Great Shepherd of the sheep give us grace to be faithful under-shepherds, to seek the lost sheep, to lead and feed the flock, to nurture the precious lambs, to protect them from the wolves, and to help them mature to the glory of God.

Warren W. Wiersbe,
Senior Pastor
MOODY MEMORIAL CHURCH
CHICAGO, ILLINOIS

JANUARY 1973

Chapter 1

The Shepherd Idea in Scripture and History

Of all the titles which have been chosen for the envoys of the Son of God, that of "shepherd" is the most popular, the most beautiful, and the most ample. Bishop, presbyter, preacher, priest, clergyman, rector, parson, minister—all of these have been long, and are still in use, but not one of them is so satisfying or sufficient as "shepherd."

"Bishop" came into the church from the Gentile world, and was early set aside to designate a special grade of minister—thus losing the range of application which it formerly possessed. In the original sense of the word, a bishop is one who oversees and superintends. The head, therefore, of every congregation might be rightfully called a bishop. Such use of it under present conditions would be misleading.

"Presbyter" came into the church through Judaism. Because both the Jewish and Gentile worlds are reflected in our New Testament, presbyter and bishop stand side by side upon its pages. At the beginning, bishop and presbyter were synonymous titles belonging to one and the same official. In time, however, the bishops of the local church dropped the title "bishop," that name being borne thereafter solely by the heads of dioceses or districts. "Presbyter," the name retained by the head of the local congregation, carries, in addition, the idea of age. Only men of years could be elders in the Jewish church. In the Christian church, age is not a prime qualification for office, or an essential possession of those who lead. The word "elder" does not emphasize that which is cardinal in Christian work; it calls attention to the years a man has lived rather than to the work which he has been called to do.

"Priest" is a title borrowed from both Judaism and Paganism, and around it ages of controversy have raged. It has always been contended by many that the idea of priest is foreign to the Christian religion, and that to call the head of a Christian church a priest is to introduce a concept which works mischief. It is significant that both Jesus and his apostles carefully avoid that word. Only sects or sections of the church of Christ today make use of it.

"Preacher" is also a sectional title, confined to those areas of the Christian world in which preaching is considered the chief if not the only heaven-ordained work of an ambassador of Christ. The use of such a title implies that the head of a church is preeminently a speaker, and that in the act of speaking he is performing the crowning function of his office. "Clergyman" is a rather chilling name, fixing the mind not on the man's personality but on his office. "Rector" is to many a repellent title, magnifying as it does the idea of ruling, and carrying with it unpleasant reminiscences of days when ecclesiastical leaders of despotic temper lorded it over the saints of God.

"Parson," the favorite title of George Herbert and of many others, has in our modern world taken on a somewhat depreciatory color. When men speak facetiously of the minister they usually call him "parson," with a familiar accent which patronizes and smiles. The word "parson" is really the word "person," and in times when the representative of the church was the one august and imperial person in the parish, there was a fitness in the title which it has long since lost. In these democratic days when the minister has stepped down from his pedestal, it is usually mock reverence which toys with the title "parson." Parson has become a sort of joke.

"Minister" is, on the whole, a wider and more adequate title than any of the seven already mentioned, but it has the disadvantage of being the same title by which the State names the highest of its officials. When one speaks of the "minister," it is impossible from that word alone for the hearer to decide whether it is a minister of the church or a minister of the government to whom reference is made. One of the limitations of the name is its ambiguity, and another is its failure to discriminate. It does not distinguish the leader from his followers. It does not draw a line between the general and his soldiers. It is a word which properly belongs to every follower of Jesus. Servantship is the essence of the Christian life. All Christians are ministers or servants. To speak of "the minister" is to imply that there is only one, whereas there ought to be as many as there are members of the church. One wonders sometimes whether the rank and file of our churches would not have been more zealous in ministering to one another and also to the community if the name "minister" had not been monopolized by a single man. The exclusive use of the title seems to justify indolent church members in their habit of considering the pastor the only obligated church worker.

But when we come to "shepherd," which is the actual meaning of the word "pastor," we reach a title without spot or wrinkle or any such thing. Here is a word which has come down through the centuries without loss of meaning and free from stain. It is the one title which is prized and reverenced in every fold of the great flock of Christ. In the Greek and Roman and Anglican communions, in the Lutheran, Reformed, and other great Christian bodies, "pastor" is a name which gives no offense. Rome likes the word. Her priests in charge of churches are called "pastors."

The Church of England likes the word; she calls her rectors "pastors." Churches which usually call their leaders ministers and preachers call them also "pastors," unwilling to part with so glorious a name. "Pastor" is a word understood around the world. In this ancient title the Church of Christ is beautifully united. Like the Lord's Prayer and the Ten Commandments, it is a treasure which no company of Christian people is willing to let go. Divisions have never laid their hands upon it. Many precious inheritances have been torn to pieces, but this remains unimpaired. When the time for the reunion of Christendom arrives, and good men begin to ask what name shall be given to those servants of the Lord to whom is entrusted the guidance of the local congregations, who can doubt that the word to be agreed upon will be the very word which the Lord chose for himself when he said: "I am the Good Shepherd."

One of the secrets of the fascination of "shepherd" as a title is that the word carries us straight to Christ himself. It associates us at once with him. So far as the New Testament tells us, Jesus never called himself a priest, or a preacher, or a rector, or a clergyman, or a bishop, or an elder, but he liked to think of himself as a shepherd. The shepherd idea was often in his mind. When he looked out upon the crowds in Galilee, they reminded him of sheep without a shepherd. He told men repeatedly that he had been sent to

gather and save the lost sheep of the House of
Israel. He considered his followers sheep, and
looking into the distance, he saw other sheep
which also were his own. "Other sheep I have,
which are not of this fold: them also I must bring,
and they shall hear my voice; and they shall become one flock, one shepherd." When he thought
of himself in the world to come, seated on a
throne with all the nations assembled before him,
even there he was still a shepherd, doing things
which shepherds do.

Early in Hebrew history, the word "shepherd"
had become a metaphor. The keeper of sheep was
so prominent a character in those early days that
he became a type of the highest servant of Jehovah, a symbol for the expression of lofty ideals
of service. Fragrant memories gathered round the
word, and men associated with it rare and precious meanings. A priest was called a shepherd,
and so also was a prophet, and so also later on
was a prince or king. Every man in an exalted
place, entrusted with public responsibilities, was
crowned with the title "shepherd." So beautiful
was the figure and so rich its content, that by and
by somebody applied it even to God. Kings and
princes, priests and prophets here on earth were
under-shepherds, and in the heavens there was
a shepherd over all—Jehovah. A poetic genius
taught all his countrymen to sing: "The Lord is
my shepherd, I shall not want." When the nation
fell into difficulties and calamities overtook it, the

saints cried out: "Give ear, O Shepherd of Israel, thou that leadest Joseph like a flock." Before men dared to think of God as their Father, they called him their Shepherd. Divine shepherdhood was one of the steps in the shining stairway up which the world climbed to the idea of divine father-hood.

But while there was a good Shepherd in the skies, there was no good shepherd on the earth. All the shepherds of Israel, one after another, proved disappointing. They did not do their duty. They failed to feed the flock. They did not wisely guide it. They could not save it. But the Hebrew heart did not despair. It dared to dream of an ideal shepherd who would surely come. A Mes-siah had been promised, and he would be a shep-herd. He would guide and feed and save the sheep. Through many generations this figure of the Shepherd-Messiah flitted before the minds of the seers of Israel. They painted him in colors which at last burned themselves into the retina of the nation's eyes. When they painted pictures of bad shepherds, they always hung up another picture, the picture of the shepherd who was good. When they wished to criticize an unworthy king or condemn an unfaithful priest, they com-pared him with the shepherd whom God had promised. It was this portrait of the good shep-herd which sustained the nation's heart. "He will feed his flock like a shepherd. He will gather the lambs in his arms and carry them in his bosom,

and will gently lead those that have their young."
Thus did they contrast the Shepherd-Messiah
with the shepherds who had been impatient and
selfish and cruel. It was to men whose eyes were
filled with this lovely picture and whose hearts
were awed by this thrilling expectation that Jesus
spoke when he said: "I am the good shepherd.
Thieves and robbers have preceded me, men who
have done all the abominations which Ezekiel
and Zechariah and others have narrated, but I
am the good shepherd. I know every sheep by
name. I give security and liberty and sustenance
to all. I am going to lay down my life for the
sheep." Jesus had many metaphors by which to
explain his character and his office, but the metaphor by which he loved best to paint his portrait
was "shepherd."

As he chose this title for himself, so also did he
give it to the leader of the apostles. Peter was a
fisherman and could have best understood, pre-
sumably, the language native to a fisherman's
lips, but Jesus in his final charge to the son of
Jonas used only the vocabulary of the sheepfold:
"Feed my lambs. Tend my sheep. Feed my
sheep." In other words: "Be a shepherd, and do
a shepherd's work." The great Shepherd of the
sheep, in framing a charge which he deemed sufficient for the guidance and encouragement of
the leaders of the Christian church to the end of
time, used only a shepherd's speech. The history
of the church begins with Jesus saying to the

leader who was to head the work of discipling the nations: "I am a shepherd, be thou a shepherd too."

Peter never forgot what the Lord said to him that morning down on the shore of the sea. Like the Master, he looked at men henceforth always with a shepherd's eyes. "Ye were going astray like sheep," he writes to a company of his converts, "but are now returned unto the Shepherd and Bishop of your souls." It was the Good Shepherd who had found Peter, and who had given him his work. It is the Good Shepherd for whose return the apostle waits. The Supreme Shepherd is coming again; therefore Peter writes to the pastors of the churches: "Tend the flock of God which is among you. Make yourselves examples to the flock, and when the Chief Shepherd shall be manifested, ye shall receive the crown of glory that fadeth not away." Peter did all of his work, not under a great taskmaster's eye, but under the gentle and loving glance of the Shepherd whose delight it is to seek and to save that which is lost.

Paul was not one of the original twelve. He never knew Jesus in the flesh, but he received from him by the Spirit the idea of shepherding. Paul, like Peter, loved to think of himself as a shepherd. He looked upon men with the loving solicitude and searching affection of a shepherd's eyes. Every church was to him a fold, and the men in charge of the church were shepherds. He speaks to the officers of the church in Ephesus in the language of a shepherd: "Take heed unto yourselves, and to all the flock, to feed the church of the Lord which he purchased with his own blood. In all things I gave you an example."

The shepherd idea, then, may be said to color the entire New Testament world, to permeate its atmosphere and to flow in its blood. The generation of Christians molded by the apostles was trained to think of Jesus as the Good Shepherd, and the church leaders instructed by Peter and Paul went forth as shepherds to feed and tend Christ's sheep. It is a ruling idea of the apostolic age which breaks into music in the fullest-toned of all our New Testament benedictions: "Now the God of peace, who brought again from the dead the Great Shepherd of the sheep with the blood of an eternal covenant, even our Lord Jesus, make you perfect in every good thing to do his will, working in us that which is well-pleasing in his sight, through Jesus Christ; to whom be glory for ever and ever. Amen." This is the benediction which the New Testament pronounces over all Christian workers, and it has a special significance for men who are fitting themselves for service in the Christian ministry. It is through the Great Shepherd of the sheep that God perfects men for the doing of his will. It is by building up in them a shepherd's disposition and imparting to them a shepherd's skill that he enables them to do that which is well-pleasing in his sight. If the aim of our life is to be Christlike, then we must be like a shepherd. If we are called to fulfill Christ's mission, then our work is that of a shepherd. If we are to be judged by Christ, then the standard of the judgment day is to be the standard of a shepherd. Since Christ is the image of his Father, it follows that God himself is a Shepherd God. To glorify him we must do a shepherd's work, and to enjoy him forever we must have the shepherd heart.

• • •

It is an interesting fact that when we close the New Testament and look about for books created by the post-apostolic age, almost the first volume which comes to hand is a little treatise, a sort of Bunyan's *Pilgrim's Progress*, a book which almost won for itself a place in the canon of our New Testament, and which for a long time was read in Christian churches, quoted in Christian sermons, and expounded in Christian books as though it were a part of authentic Scripture— "The Shepherd of Hermas." It is a curious little pamphlet, and everybody is glad now that it did not succeed in establishing itself in our Bible. But it contains much that is suggestive, and one of its interesting features is that Hermas got his instruction and inspiration from a shepherd.

The scholars tell us that in the oldest of the catacombs the favorite Christian figure is that of a shepherd. He is in the bloom of youth, with a crook or a shepherd's pipe in one hand, and on his shoulder a lamb which he carefully holds with the other hand. Sometimes he is attended by one sheep only, at other times by two. Often there are several sheep at his feet in various attitudes. It was a shepherd whom these early Christians loved to paint on the walls of their chapels and oratories, and to chisel on the tombs of their dead. They engraved the image of the shepherd on the chalices which they used at the sacrament of the Last Supper. They traced it in gold on the glasses from which they drank at their feasts; they molded it on lamps, carved it on rings, painted it in frescoes upon the walls of the chambers of death, carved it on tablets, sculptured it on sarcophagi. It is found on thousands of tombs. It was the first favorite symbol of Christian life and faith. In this way we become certain what the second-century Christians thought of Jesus. This figure of the shepherd reveals how they regarded him in their deepest experiences, in what form he comforted them in their most solemn hours. It was the tenderness of the shepherd which soothed them when their hearts were bleeding. It was the shepherd's courage and strength which braced them in the day of persecution and in the hour of death. Christianity was at first the religion of the Good Shepherd.

To the men of the second century the Savior of the world was a keeper of sheep. As Dean Stanley says, "The kindness, the courage, the grace, the love, the beauty of the Good Shepherd was to them prayer book and articles, creed and canons, all in one. They looked on that figure and it conveyed to them all that they wanted. As ages passed on, the Good Shepherd faded away from the mind of the Christian world, and other emblems of the Christian faith have taken his place. Instead of the gracious and gentle Pastor, there came the omnipotent Judge, or the crucified Sufferer, or the Infant in his mother's arms, or the Master in his parting supper, or the figures of innumerable saints and angels, or the elaborate expositions of the various forms of theological controversy. There is hardly any allusion to the Good Shepherd in Athanasius or in Jerome. There is hardly any in the *Summa Theologiae* of Thomas Aquinas, none in the Trindentine catechism, none in the Thirty-nine Articles, none in the Westminster Confession."

When church leaders began to lose the vision of the Good Shepherd, they at the same time began to drift away from the New Testament ideal of ministerial service. Little by little they magnified their office in ways not sanctioned by the Good Shepherd of the sheep. They became priests offering a bloodless sacrifice; they assumed the functions of rulers, making a specialty of law and discipline. They degenerated into tyrants, setting themselves up as sole custodians of the grace of God, claiming sovereignty not only over the kingdoms of this world but also over the vast empire of the dead. The church lost the way which leads to life as soon as the envoys of the Son of God forgot that they were shepherds. Darkness fell upon the earth when the shepherd was swallowed up in the priest.

But an ideal, once apprehended, never fades completely from the mind of the world. The church has never surrendered entirely her belief in Jesus as the Shepherd Savior, and has never given up altogether her feeling that ministers ought to be shepherds of the sheep. The shepherd idea has something in it which appeals to the universal heart. Even in our Western world from which machinery and commerce have driven the shepherd and his flock, the best-loved of all the psalms remains the Shepherd Psalm. More men and women read and cherish "The Lord is my shepherd, I shall not want" than any other poem in the Psalter. Millions who have had no experience with sheepfolds, and to whom a sheep has been an animal almost unknown, have been strangely moved by the piercing pathos of the story which Jesus told of a shepherd who went out in search of one sheep that was lost. What Christian song went deeper into the heart of the nineteenth century than "There were ninety and nine that safely lay in the shelter of the fold" as sung by Mr. Sankey round the world? Congregations every Sunday sing:

Savior, like a shepherd lead us,
  Much we need Thy tender care;

In Thy pleasant pastures feed us;
  For our use Thy folds prepare,

and also this:
  In tenderness he sought me,
    Weary and weak with sin;
  And on his shoulders brought me
    Back to his fold again,

and also this:
  The King of love my Shepherd is,
    Whose goodness faileth never;
  I nothing lack if I am his
    And he is mine forever.

Into the prayers as well as the hymnology, the shepherd idea has been inextricably woven. Multitudes of hearts find relief in making the confession: "We have erred and strayed from thy ways like lost sheep. We have followed too much the devices and desires of our own hearts." The devout heart drops unconsciously into such phrases as "All we like sheep have gone astray; we have turned every one to his own way; and Jehovah hath laid on him the iniquity of us all." The Spirit in us, helping our infirmities, teaches us to cry out: "O thou Great Shepherd of the sheep! Guide us, feed us, save us evermore!"

It is necessary only to walk through any of the great European picture galleries to see what an impression the shepherd idea has made on the mind of the artist. Masters of the brush have ever loved to paint Jesus as a shepherd. Wherever that picture is displayed, human eyes are attracted by it and human hearts are ministered to. The heart of a man is like the heart of a sheep: it beats at the sight of a shepherd.

The shepherd idea has worked its way deep into Christian literature. It has molded, more than we think, not only the language but the thought of the Christian church. Do we not speak of the pastoral epistles? And have we not in every theological seminary a Chair of Pastoral Theology? And do we not have at our ordinations pastoral charges? Is not one of the most famous of all recent Encyclicals of the Pope entitled, "The Feeding of the Flock"? The shepherd concept haunts us, clings to us, will not let us go. This is the Lord's doing, and it ought to be marvelous in our eyes. Blessed is the man who ponders its significance and allows it to teach him what it has to tell. We lose something by confining the Anglo-Saxon word "shepherd" to the fields, and shutting up the Latin word "pastor" in the church. We know with our intellect that the two words are synonymous, but we forget it often with our hearts. It would help us to say occasionally, "The Lord is my Pastor." It would lift the word "pastor" to higher dignity, and pour into it a more heavenly meaning. It would chasten and strengthen every minister of Christ if now and then he would say to himself, "I am a shepherd. My work is the herding and feeding of sheep." Self-condemnation would come to more than one pastor if his people should begin someday to speak of him as "our shepherd."

There is danger in a time like this that the shepherd concept may become obscured. Just as the shepherd idea was swallowed up in the priest idea, causing a blight to fall upon the church, so a calamity of another sort is sure to overtake us if the shepherd idea is swallowed up in the preacher idea. A Roman Catholic boy intended for the priesthood is always looking forward to the time when he can officiate at the mass. The day on which he celebrates his first mass is a red-letter day in his life. A Catholic boy thinks that the chief work of a minister of Christ is to perform a ceremony—offering up to God a wafer which has become in some inexplicable way the body of God's Son. That false idea demoralizes and darkens the entire Roman Catholic world. The Protestant boy intending to enter the ministry looks forward to the day when he will preach his first sermon. The date of the event is a cardinal day on his calendar. Protestant ministers to the end of their life talk about their first sermon, just as Roman Catholic priests talk to the final sunset about their first mass. Both men are alike in putting the supreme emphasis on a public performance—the one on a ceremony, the other on a discourse. The one makes the altar, the other makes the pulpit, the holy of holies of the Chris-

tian church. The one thinks the world is blessed
by converting the wafer into the body of Christ,
the other that humanity is advanced by his ex-
position of the life and ideas of Jesus. Both are
mistaken. The New Testament truth knows neither the altar nor the pulpit. The first elders and
bishops were not preachers in our sense of that
word, and it was not for generations that the
Lord's Supper was converted into the mass. The
first permanent officials of the local congregations
in the days of the apostles were overseers, su-
perintendents, guides, presbyters, bishops—in
other words, pastors, herders of the sheep. The
pastoral idea is deeper than the priest idea or the
preacher idea, and it is also wider. Its contents
are richer. Priests and preachers impoverish their
lives and curtail their usefulness when they fail
to keep alive in their hearts the shepherd idea.

The pastoral notion is disparaged, not only by
many ministers, but also by most of our churches.
Our Protestant churches look first of all for what
they call a preacher, a man who is an expert
speaker and who can draw and hold a company
of listeners. Who ever heard of a man being called
to a church because he was a good shepherd! The
popular estimate of pastoral service comes out
also in the policy adopted by the church in doing
its work. No man can truly be the pastor of more
than a few hundred people, and yet churches roll
up their membership sometimes to a thousand
while that one man is expected to go on doing all

the work of the church. The result is he can do nothing well. He is a failure as a pastor, and sooner or later he breaks down as a preacher. Every city church of a thousand members ought to have a staff of pastors; each one ought to do the thing he can do the best. We ought to utilize in the ministry men of the most diverse endowments. We impoverish our church life by limiting the ministry practically to men of a single type.

Nearly all our city churches are run on the old village plan: one man is supposed to do everything. No wonder they do not cope successfully with city problems. A village church in a city environment is impotent. Men and money are being squandered in a senseless effort to do the impossible. What our city churches need more than all things else is *pastors*. A city church, like a city hospital or city school, is an expensive institution and laymen must be educated to pour their money into it with a generosity hitherto unknown. It is because Christian laymen as a rule do not know the value of pastoral service that so many of our city churches are today fighting a losing battle.

When at last the membership becomes unwieldy, and the pastor is seen to stagger under his load, and in sheer desperation the church decides to obtain the services of a second worker, who is that second worker likely to be? Some young man, perhaps just out of seminary, who is willing to work for his clothes and board, or some aged saint whose waning vitality has closed to him every other door. For the pulpit, everybody is certain that a man must have brains, talent, genius; but for pastoral service it is a common impression that almost any man is sufficient. The churches show their estimate of pastoral service by the policy they pursue in securing it.

The schools of theology have been in some measure responsible for the ignorance of the churches. A glance at the curriculum of the old-fashioned seminary is sufficient to show that pastoral theology was, in the judgment of the doctors, a subordinate branch of knowledge. Greek and Hebrew, comparative religion, the confessions and creeds, sacred rhetoric and elocution, homiletics in all of its branches, systems of theology—surely these have had the uppermost seats at the theological feasts, and young men have been trained not to scoff at pastoral work but to place it in a subordinate rank. Spiritual therapeutics, moral ethics, the cure of souls, the remedies provided in the Christian pharmacopeia, the application of Christian principles to specific ailments of the individual heart—surely these are studies which have received less than their deserts. Then again, the science of sociology, the art of cooperation, the philosophy of fellowship—all of those knowledges and disciplines involving social life and communal action have been too often slighted, if not completely ignored.

Many a seminary graduate, floundering amid the complicated forces of his first church, has cried out in humiliation and anger: "Why did they not teach me in the seminary how to organize my work and how to grapple with all this mass of tangled and critical problems for whose solution I am totally unprepared?"

One result of this disparagement of pastoral service is visible in the sentiments entertained by many young men entering the ministry. They say quite openly that they despise pastoral work. Study they enjoy, books they love, preaching they revel in. But as for shepherding the sheep, they hate it. They like to feel that they have special gifts for the pulpit. When their friends prophesy for them a glorious pulpit career, their heart sings. The work of the shepherd was an abomination, we are told, to the ancient Egyptians, and so it is to all pulpit-Pharaohs who are interested in building pyramids out of eloquent words. The fear of failing in pastoral duty is never once before their eyes. A slip in the pulpit brings gnawing remorse; a blunder in pastoral work gives the conscience not a twinge. Public worship is to them the be-all and the end-all of ministerial life. They have not read the New Testament sufficiently to observe that public worship is not made the one thing needful, either by Jesus or the apostles; and that while it is not to be neglected, there are many weightier matters of the law.

In defense of young men who look askance at

pastoral work, it may be said that youth is the time when the intellect is voracious for ideas and when God intends men to furnish their minds. Young men are, if intellectually alert, interested more in ideas than in men. Moreover, the gift of speech is a gift early developed, and the love of speaking is one of the delights of youth. Shepherding sheep, one at a time, cannot be expected to be so fascinating to young men as blowing a thrilling message through a silver trumpet in the ears of a crowd on the Lord's Day. Moreover, young ministers have the peculiar frailties which are inseparable from youth. They like commendation. They are sensitive to applause. They are fond of the limelight—how can they help it? They are encouraged by attention in the public press.* Papers are everywhere, and their contents are discussed in every circle. To get into the papers, therefore, is one way for a minister to multiply his power. And to get into the papers a man must preach. He can say things in the pulpit which the reporters will be glad to print. He can accomplish things from the pulpit which the world needs to have done. Young men are rightfully ambitious to make their lives count for the most possible. They are commendably eager to gain attention for their message. The pulpit is a sort of housetop from which they can shout their tidings to all the town. In pastoral work, however, a man is on the ground, and the world is

---

* This, of course, was before the days of radio and television, today's avenue to public acclaim. *Editor*

not likely to pay attention to him.

Again, youth is naturally impatient. It wants things done, and it wants them done at once. To deal with men one at a time is tedious and exhausting. To coax one bad boy into obedience to his mother, or to lift one slave of drink into sobriety and freedom, or to brighten one humble household with a smile and a prayer—this requires patience and tact and sacrifice, and it seems puttering work compared with making a great hit with a crowd of people all at once on the Lord's Day. Youth longs to do things in haste, and for this we should not be sorry. It is the glory of a young man that he wants to move fast, and that he is not so patient with things as they are, as an old man is. It is a certain burning swiftness of the blood which makes many a young man averse to pastoral work.

There are certain gifts and graces which, like the oak, mature but slowly. One of these is sympathy. Sympathy is the outgrowth of experience. The experience of young men is limited, and for this they are not to blame. Many a young man has been sorely troubled on entering his first church because of his feeble love for people. On examining his heart he has found it cold and dead. He has looked at the men and women before him and confessed to himself that for most of them he does not care. There seems to be no point of contact between him and them. He has been studying and they have simply been existing. They know hardly anything and he knows a lot. He has been thinking; they do not seem to have thought at all. He is quite familiar with all the great thinkers of Germany and of England and Scotland, but in his group these kings of modern thought are quite unknown. The very wisest of his people do not know what Ritschlianism is, or Pragmatism, or Vitalism, or Monism, or Modernism, or anything else worth the attention of the modern man. The men in his church are simply buying and selling, working and playing. The women are keeping house and fulfilling various social functions. The world is eating and drinking, marrying and giving in marriage, very much as it did before the Flood. How is it possible for a young man reared in the world of books to take a hearty and genuine interest at once in a world so stupid and backward? It is by no means easy for a young man to become a shepherd, and he ought not to be discouraged if he cannot become one in a day, or a year. An orator he can be without difficulty. A reformer he can become at once. In criticism of politics and society he can do a flourishing business the first Sunday. But a shepherd he can become only slowly, and by patiently traveling the way of the cross.

The shepherd's work is a humble work; such it has been from the beginning and such it must be to the end. A man must come down to do it. A shepherd cannot shine. He cannot cut a figure. His work must be done in obscurity. The things which he does do not make interesting copy. His work calls for continuous self-effacement. It is a form of service which eats up a man's life. It makes a man old before his time. Every good shepherd lays down his life for the sheep. If a man is dependent on the applause of the crowd, he ought never to enter the ministry. The finest things a minister does are done out of sight and never get reported. They are known to himself and one or two others, and to God. His joy is not that his success is being talked about on earth, but that his name is written in heaven. The shepherd in the East had no crowd to admire him. He lived alone with the sheep and the stars. His satisfactions were from within. The messengers of Christ must not expect bands of music to attend them on their way. Theirs is humble, unpretentious, and oftentime unnoticed labor, but if it builds souls in righteousness it is more lasting than the stars.

How, then, can a young man with limited experience, undeveloped sympathies, an impatient temper, a longing for attention, a love of self-expression and a passion for ideas, become a true shepherd of his people? First of all let him study afresh the life of the ideal Shepherd, and then let him day by day, both by prayer and self-sacrificing deeds, endeavor to build up in himself the mind of Christ. "Pains and prayers through Jesus Christ can accomplish anything," John Eliot wrote long ago. Jesus was a young man, but he had the shepherd heart. Nearness to him is the indispensable condition of absorbing the shepherd temperament and learning the shepherd ways.

A careful student of the New Testament does not fail to note how careful the Evangelists are to state the scope of Jesus' work and the range of the duties which he lays upon the twelve. Luke tells us that Jesus in his first sermon in Nazareth accepted the program laid down by Isaiah, and this program was to preach good tidings to the poor and proclaim release to the captives, to bring about recovery of sight to the blind, to set at liberty them that are bruised, and to proclaim the acceptable year of the Lord. Speech and action are combined. The Messiah is both to teach and to do. Luke never loses sight of this twofold work. He tells Theophilus that his Gospel is the story of what Jesus began both to do and to teach until the day on which he was received up. He says that to the twelve Jesus gave a twofold work. He called the twelve together and gave them power and authority over all demons and to cure diseases, and he sent them forth to preach the kingdom of God and to heal the sick. The twelve understood that they were to do more than preach. They departed and went throughout the villages preaching the gospel and healing everywhere. In our oldest Gospel, Mark, the same distinction is made clear. "He appointed twelve that they might be with him, and that he might send them forth to preach and to have authority to cast out demons." This was the work which he himself had been doing. He went into their synagogues throughout all Galilee, "preaching and casting out demons." Matthew maintains the same distinction. "Jesus went about all the cities and the villages, teaching in their synagogues and preaching the gospel of the kingdom, and healing all manner of disease and all manner of sickness." It was when Jesus saw the multitudes distressed and scattered as sheep not having a shepherd that "he called unto him his twelve disciples, and gave them authority over unclean spirits, to cast them out, and to heal all manner of disease and all manner of sickness." In other words, the twelve were not simply to proclaim in general phrases a message for the crowd; they were to preach and they were to deal with men one by one, casting out their evil spirits and healing their diseases.

If, then, we are the successors of the apostles, we must have the apostolic spirit and do the apostles' work. We must shepherd the multitudes who are distressed and scattered, and bring the life and love of God by our own Spirit-filled personality into the mind and heart of the individual. It is only by pastoral work that the world can be saved.

Without pastoral work the minister himself cannot be saved. If salvation is health, and health is the kind of life which we find in Jesus of Nazareth, then how can a minister be in sound health who lacks the shepherd heart, and how can he have peace and joy if he shirks the shepherd's responsibilities and runs away from the shepherd's crosses? The finest test of the consecration of a minister of Christ is not in his public performances but in what he does when the world is not looking. It is hard for a man to tell, when he is preaching, whether he is preaching for himself or for God. To open up glorious ideas, to clothe them with language which glows and speak them in tones which burn—all this is so delightful that it is not easy for the preacher to say just why he likes to do it. But in the obscurity of pastoral service he has opportunity to ascertain whether he really loves God and how much he is willing to do for people simply for Jesus' sake.

A minister can skimp his pastoral work and still retain his position as the shepherd of the flock, but he cannot retain his robust position in God's kingdom. The unfaithful shepherd is punished by a penalty automatically inflicted and inescapable. Little by little his conscience is deadened, the heart becomes less sensitive, the spiritual eye loses its keenness, and the culprit, still outwardly devout and publicly honored, is pushed slowly but inexorably by the hand of the Almighty into deeper depths of that darkness of soul prepared for all who are recreant to their trust. Men shirk pastoral service not because they are strong, but because they are weak. They have not sufficient strength to bend their life to the life of Christ. It is the weaklings and not the giants who neglect their people. It is the pagan and not the Christian who shines in public and leaves undone the private duties which belong to him as an ordained steward of the Son of God. When a man says, "I hate pastoral work, and do as little of it as I can"—if he had ears to hear, he could hear the Spirit saying: "Thou fool!"

A few things are certain. We live in a universe created by a Shepherd God. The Lord is our Shepherd. Our world is redeemed by a Shepherd Savior. Our Elder Brother is a Shepherd. The man whom humanity most needs is a shepherd. Every messenger of Christ is sent to do a shepherd's work. We are to stand at last before a Shepherd Judge. God is going to separate the good shepherds from the shepherds who are bad. The questions which every pastor must meet and answer are three: "Did you feed my lambs? Did you tend my sheep? Did you feed my sheep?"

2

THE SHEPHERD'S WORK

One reason why pastoral work is frequently disparaged is because the conception of it has been unwarrantably narrowed. By robbing it of breadth, it is easy to make it look insignificant. Pastoral dignity is inevitably lowered by every curtailment of the range of pastoral responsibility.

What is pastoral work? A common answer is that it is presiding at marriages and also at funerals. It is baptizing babies and saying a kind word to strangers. It is comforting the sick and helping the poor. He who does these things faithfully is a good pastor. Such is the popular conception. But if this is the bulk of pastoral work, how meager it is, and how easily it might all be done by laymen. If to these six universally recognized pastoral functions there be added the task of systematic pastoral visitation, such as is expected in many Protestant churches, the rounded whole of a pastor's work is supposed to be set forth. But concerning the utility of this pastoral visitation there is widespread skepticism, and against it there is constant revolt. Who has not heard scornful things said about the foolishness of wasting time in ringing doorbells and filling up the afternoon with a round of social calls which exhaust the minister and add nothing to the spiritual welfare of his people? By some the work of pastoral visitation may be counted easy. Preaching, of course, is labor, but pastoral calling is recreation—sort of ministerial play. To others it is not play but tribulation—an exhausting drudgery, a cruel infliction visited on helpless ministers, sanctioned by tradition but not included in the plan of God. It is because men do not see clearly what pastoral service really is that such service is often scorned and slighted. A few items of parochial administration are seized upon and made the sum total of the pastor's labor. Anything becomes contemptible if you whittle it down to a splinter. The seven functions above referred to are only minor fractions of a pastor's toil.

Pastoral work does not appeal to a large and noble mind until it is seen in its entirety, and until the wealth of its opportunity and the manifoldness of its responsibility are clearly apprehended. To find out the scope of pastoral service, we must go to the area where our shepherd metaphor was born and ascertain what was in Palestine a shepherd's work. Jesus was an Asian. He spoke to Asians. He thought in terms familiar to the Asian mind. He belonged to a nation whose wealth was largely in sheep, and over the fields of whose history there came constantly the lowing of cattle and the bleating of lambs. Some of the greatest of the Hebrew heroes had been keepers of sheep. All of the patriarchs, the greatest of the lawgivers, the sweetest of the poets, and some of the mightiest of the prophets had in early life been shepherds. To Hebrew eyes the work of shepherding had a glory invisible to our eyes. In Palestine, and in the countries round about, a shepherd's work was by no means simple or easy. It was arduous and manifold. It called into exercise varied faculties, it gave scope for the exhibition of the loftiest virtues. It taxed the higher range of talents and developed the noblest qualities of the soul. By glancing at the range of the shepherd's duties we shall be able to comprehend what pastoral service meant to Jesus, why he phrased his charge to the chief of the apostles in the vocabulary of the sheepfold, and how it came to pass that the title chosen by him for himself was "Shepherd."

I. The Eastern shepherd was, first of all, a watchman. He had a watchtower. It was his business to keep a wide-open eye, constantly searching the horizon for the possible approach of foes. He was bound to be circumspect and attentive. Vigilance was a cardinal virtue. An alert wakefulness was for him a necessity. He could not indulge in fits of drowsiness, for the foe was always near. Only by his alertness could the enemy be circumvented. There were many kinds of enemies, all of them terrible, each in a different way. At certain seasons of the year there were floods. Streams became quickly swollen and overflowed their banks. Swift action was necessary in order to escape destruction. There were enemies of a more subtle kind—animals, rapacious and treacherous: lions, bears, hyenas, jackals, wolves. There were enemies in the air—huge birds of prey were always soaring aloft, ready to swoop down upon a lamb or kid. And then, most dangerous of all, were the human birds and beasts of prey—robbers, bandits, men who made a business of robbing sheepfolds and murdering shepherds. That Eastern world was full of perils. It teemed with forces hostile to the shepherd and his flock. When Ezekiel, Jeremiah, Isaiah and Habakkuk talk about shepherds, they call them watchmen set to warn and save.

The first great pastor of the Christian church, Paul, in his farewell address to the officers of the church in Ephesus, emphasizes the importance of the work of watching. His closing exhortation is "Watch!" He gives these men a reason for his warning. Grievous wolves, he says, are going to enter in among them, not sparing the flock. And moreover, from among their own selves men are going to arise, speaking perverse things and drawing away many after them. There are two quarters from which enemies are always to be expected: from the outside and also from the inside, from the world and also from the church. Not only will there be wolves in wolves' clothing, but there will also be wolves in sheep's clothing, and against both types of wolf the Christian minister must be ever on his guard. The apostle goes on to remind his converts of the example he had set for them, saying, "Remember that for the space of three years I ceased not to admonish every one night and day with tears." Watchfulness is one of the marks of the good shepherd. The writer to the Hebrews describes church officials thus: "They watch in the interest of your souls." They are going to render an account to the Great Shepherd, and therefore they are intent upon your safety. They watch with eyes that do not sleep.

How often the word "watch" was on the lips of Jesus may be inferred from its frequency on the pages of the Gospels. To Jesus, life is critical—the soul is ever in the midst of perils. The journey from the cradle to the grave is hazardous. Men are to pray and to watch. Now, if every man is surrounded by perils, if the universe is alive with forces hostile to the soul, then watchfulness becomes one of the most critical of all the pastor's responsibilities. To him precious lives are committed, lives for which he is to render an account. Watching, surveying, scanning the horizon, peering into the darkness of days not yet born, spying out the interior nature of forces which are working like insidious and poisonous leavens, calculating the advent of storms asleep as yet in the caves of coming days—all this is pastoral work, work which, alas, is not always conscientiously performed.

Many a minister fails as a pastor because he is not vigilant. He allows his church to be torn to pieces because he is half asleep. He takes it for granted that there are no wolves, no birds of prey, no robbers, and while he is drowsing the enemy arrives. False ideas, destructive interpretations, demoralizing teachings come into his group, and he never knows it. He is interested, perhaps, in literary research; he is absorbed in the discussion contained in the last theological quarterly, and does not know what his young people are reading or what strange ideas have been lodged in the heads of a group of his leading members. There are errors which are as fierce as wolves and pitiless as hyenas; they tear faith and hope and love to pieces and leave churches, once prosperous, mangled and half dead. Or it may be that new conceptions of God and the world are rising like blazing suns in the firmament of the world of thought, and the minds of the followers of Jesus are agitated and perplexed. Instruction is needed to prepare men to refute changed ideas of the Scriptures, of inspiration, and of authority; and the watchman is looking in the other direction. He has been studying the past, he is wedded to the antique, he is a devotee at the altars of the preceding generation. He does not see that the old order is changing, giving way to new. And because he does not know what is going on in the world and in his parish, the faith of noble saints of God is being shaken and the peace of many hearts destroyed. Watching is one of the chief forms of pastoral service. A pastor is a watchman. His home is to be a tower.

II. A shepherd in the East was also a guard. His mission was not only to oversee, it was likewise to protect. He was a guardian of the sheep. He was their defender. Sheep are among the most defenseless of animals. They are not provided with weapons of attack or defense. They can neither bite nor scratch nor kick. They can run, but not as fast as their enemies. A sheep is no match for many an animal half its size. Its helplessness is pitiable. It is dependent absolutely on human strength and wisdom. Its safety lies entirely in man. Man is its refuge, its buckler, its shield, its rock, its fortress. Everything that the Psalmist calls God, a sheep might call its shepherd. The walls of the sheepfold are built by the shepherd. When there are no stones, he builds thorn bushes into barriers. The door of the sheepfold is made by him, opened and closed by him. By his foresight the sheep are protected. By his courage they are saved. He defends them in the hour of attack. He safeguards them when they are not aware of danger. They owe their safety to him when they are least conscious of their obligation. The shepherd in the East was a guard, a protector, a defender. "Though I walk through the valley of deep darkness, I will fear no evil, for thou art with me." The ravine or deep gorge in the East was the hiding-place of wild animals and the resort of dangerous men. Even here, however, the sheep were secure when the shepherd was with them. His rod and his staff protected them.

The safeguarding of the sheep is a prime function in pastoral work. How to protect the young men of the community from overwhelming temptation, how to shelter the girls of a village or city from unnecessary dangers, how to shield the wage earner from the gambling den and the liquor saloon, how to keep amusements and recreations from degenerating into forms of demoralization, how to curtail evils which cannot be annihilated, and how to guard boys and girls against influences which stain the mind and eat out the bloom of the heart; all this work of prevention is pastoral work, and what work is more important and more difficult? To create obstructions in the stream of evil, to build up walls against the packs of animal forces which lacerate and ruin, to erect safeguards on the brink of dangerous precipices over which thousands have fallen to their death—this is pastoral work, and it is the shame of the church that not more of it has been done.

We have spent too much time in coaxing half-dead sheep back to life again, and not time enough in building barriers against the wolves. Ministers in large numbers do not anticipate as they should the perils which their people are bound to meet. They do not take the necessary precautions for themselves or for those entrusted to their keeping. They do not plan and work for the creation of agencies for warding off attack. They do not intercept by skillful and timely measures the ruin which the enemy has plotted. There is need in every church for constructive work of the highest order. No other work demands a loftier grade of intelligence and skill. The losses of the average church are appalling, and one reason is that life is not properly protected. The shepherd has no genius for constructing sheepfolds which will keep out the wolves. He does not seem to know that it is his duty to devise means and measures for meeting and overcoming the hostile forces which are forever making warfare on the Church of Christ. He does not guard.

III. The shepherd is a guide. Sheep are not independent travelers. They must have a human conductor. They cannot go to predetermined places by themselves. They cannot start out in the morning in search of pasture and then come home at evening time. They have, apparently, no sense of direction. The greenest pasture may be only a few miles away, but the sheep left to themselves cannot find it. What animal is more incapable than a sheep? He realizes his impotence, for no animal is more docile. Where the shepherd leads, the sheep will go. He knows that the shepherd is a guide and that it is safe to follow him. The shepherd cannot drive the sheep; he must lead them. Mules and hogs can be driven, but not sheep; their nature is to follow.

In the East a lot of guidance is necessary. The pasture is often in spots and strips, and sometimes the strips and spots are far apart. Streams are not abundant, and at certain seasons the land is parched by drought. In such a country the work of guidance is difficult and urgent. The poet who thought of God as a Shepherd knew well a shepherd's work. He thought of God first of all as a leader. God goes ahead and finds the streams which are sweet and the pastures which are fragrant. "He maketh me to lie down in green pastures. He leadeth me beside still waters." This idea of leadership was in Jesus' mind when he said: "I am the Good Shepherd." His sketch of the Palestinian shepherd was true to life. "The sheep hear his voice, and he calleth his own sheep by name and leadeth them out, and the sheep follow him for they know his voice."

It is commonplace that a minister is a leader, and yet not every minister knows how to lead. In other words, he is not a good pastor. Some ministers try to drive. Their fatal weakness is an inability to see that shepherds cannot drive. Such men are always cutting, lashing, forcing, and therefore always getting into trouble. They are continually quarreling with their people, and for no other reason than that they do not know how to lead. They push and do not draw, they shove and do not woo. They believe in propulsion and not in attraction. They lack the magic of the shepherd touch. They do not know human nature; they do not realize that men, like sheep, must be led. A minister must always go in advance of his people. He must lead them in thought. It is tragic when a minister is not the intellectual leader of his people. If his conceptions are those of the average man, if his ideas are the safe and commonplace ideas of the general community, if in his attitude to great reforms he is not in advance of the crowd, if in pulling down strongholds of evil, many are more aggressive than he, he is not a shepherd.

A minister who does not lead is shirking a capital branch of pastoral work. His people would follow if he would only lead them. But he hides himself in the middle of the flock, and often lags in the rear. Sometimes he is not a leader even in church enterprise. He does not teach his people how to work. Men and women, no matter how gifted and well meaning, do not know how to do Christian work unless instructed. The work lies all around them, but they will not take hold of it unless their hands are trained. The doors of opportunity stand open, but the average Christian will not enter unless encouraged. It is surprising how much work any congregation of Christian people will accomplish if only they have a leader. A leader is not an exhorter, or a scolder, or a declaimer, but a man who goes ahead and points out the particular things which ought to be accomplished, and not only points them out, but also shows in what manner they may best be done. Some ministers can see a huge work which ought to be attempted, but they cannot lead their people into it. They can describe critically the strategic nature of the battle that ought to be fought, but they never get their people onto the battlefield. They are visionaries, dreamers, but not shepherds. They do not lead. No one is really a leader whom men do not follow.

IV. A shepherd in Israel was a physician to the sheep. Sheep, like human beings, have diseases, and like all other living creatures on our planet, they are liable to accident and misfortune. They cut themselves, their feet get sore, they break their legs, they fall—the victims of distempers and infirmities of many kinds. The Asian shepherd was a healer of the diseases of his flock. There was usually at least one of his sheep which was lame and ailing, and upon this invalid the shepherd bestowed more abundant care. The sheep that had no appetite, the sheep that on a journey got out of breath, the sheep that limped and occasionally lay down, these were the sheep toward which the shepherd's sympathies went out. The nature of his calling compelled a shepherd to be a doctor and a nurse.

Jesus the Good Shepherd always regarded himself as a physician. He could not understand why his enemies objected to his paying attention to the sick. When he sent his disciples out, he told them both to preach and to heal, making it clear that his envoys cannot fulfill their mission by words alone; they must do a certain work.

It is the mission of the pastor to "minister to minds diseased; to pluck from the memory a rooted sorrow; to raze out the written troubles of the brain; and, with some sweet oblivious antidote, to cleanse the stuffed bosom of that perilous stuff which weighs upon the heart." There is always someone ailing in the parish, not physically only, but mentally, morally, spiritually. The diseases of the soul are numerous, and the remedies provided by the Almighty are efficacious only when applied by a skilled practitioner. There are soul diseases peculiar to certain ages and certain temperaments, to certain callings and certain environments; the minister ought to know the symptoms of these diseases, the stages of their development, and the hygienic processes by which they may be cured. There is loss of appetite, emaciation, debility, fever, blindness, deafness, palsy, paralysis, diseases of the heart, occult and baffling distempers of the mind, depression, prostration, and agonizing paroxysms of the spirit.

Here is a field in which the minister is called upon to put forth much skill and strength. His mission is to the sick, and not all sick people are sick with the same sickness, nor do they all require the same remedies or the same kind of nursing. Nowhere else does the minister need such piercing insight, such fine powers of discrimination, such skill in diagnosis and such ability to cope with subtle and mysterious forces, as here. There are ministers who hardly enter into this great realm of pastoral service. Sick consciences are in their church, but they do not know how to treat them. Wounded hearts are bleeding, but they do not know how to stop the flow of blood. Bereaved and other grief-stricken people are mourning, but they do not know how to speak the healing word. Spirits are sick unto death, but they can bring them no relief. There are those who are possessed of demons, but the pastor does not know how to cast them out. The whole science of spiritual therapeutics is unknown to him, and followers of Jesus in many cases suffer on for years with diseases from which an expert spiritual physician could have delivered them. There are in many a congregation cases of arrested religious development, instances of moral paralysis, sad attacks of spiritual prostration which could be relieved and cured if only the minister understood better the nature of the soul and the remedies offered to human minds in Jesus Christ.

There is a notion now afloat that the minister ought to take in hand all physical disorders, that he is shirking his duty if he does not widen his

province to cover all illnesses of the flesh as well
as every malady of the mind. It is undoubtedly
true that body and mind together make a man,
and that the entire man is under the law of God
and is the subject of redemption. But there is no
reason why a minister should claim to know everything or pretend to be able to do everything.
Why should he dispense with other servants of
the Almighty who are also called by heaven to
bear a share of the work of human redemption?
To the physician as well as the clergyman God
grants wisdom and grace, and to each of them is
given a part to play in the world's life and work.
It is both Christian humility and common sense
for a minister to work hand in hand with men
who have learned God's laws in other provinces
of his vast kingdom, and to avail himself of whatever help God is willing to render through them.
While the minister must not attempt to supplant
the physician, he can never without loss, however, forget that he himself as pastor is a physician, and that through all of the agencies which
God places within his reach, it is his duty to work
for the restoration of humanity to physical as well
as to spiritual health. Often the root of moral diseases is in the flesh, and many a spiritual phe-
nomenon becomes explicable only by the knowledge of physiology. The physical health of his
people is always a matter of concern to the instructed pastor. Whatever ministers to their
physical health will likewise render possible a

fuller unfolding of their spiritual nature, and a more efficient service in the kingdom of God. Hygiene—physical, moral, and spiritual—is a part of the work of the shepherd. The shepherd is the physician of the sheep.

V. The shepherd is a savior. He saves sheep that are lost. A critical part of the shepherd's task is rescue work. Sheep have a propensity for getting lost. They lose their way through stupidity and also through heedlessness and folly. A sheep will keep his nose to the ground following the strip of greenest grass, little by little separating himself from his companions, until at last, his companions completely out of sight, the poor isolated animal does not know where he is. When once he realizes his lost condition, he is furious to find his fellows. He cannot live alone; he was made for society. When by himself, he is timorous and easily panic-stricken. Every sight alarms him, every sound makes him afraid. He rushes hither and thither seeking his way, but his search is generally fruitless. A lost sheep does not get home. The more he tries to find his path, the farther is he likely to be from the fold. In his desperation he may run into a thicket or sink into a morass or fall into a pit and there perish unless the shepherd finds him. A sheep is like a man in that he cannot save himself; without a savior he is irretrievably lost.

In the Old Testament the care of the shepherd for his sheep is finely portrayed. Prophets and poets are always extolling the shepherd's care, but it is not until we pass into the New Testament that the shepherd's solicitude for the lost sheep becomes paramount and controlling. In the preaching of Jesus we get for the first time the full picture of a shepherd going out to seek the sheep that is lost. It was of this trait in shepherdhood that Jesus loved to think. This was the ruling disposition of his own great heart. When he saw the multitude he was moved with compassion for them because they were distressed, and scattered as sheep not having a shepherd. One of Jesus' sayings which the first evangelist especially loved and treasured was, "I am not sent but unto the lost sheep of the house of Israel." The shepherd who left his ninety-nine sheep in the fold and went forth in search of one sheep which had wandered away was held up by Jesus as an ideal and example. Rescue work was dear to his heart. He was always seeking the sheep that was lost. That was what he was doing the day he found Matthew in the office, and again on the day he found a woman at the well, and again on the day he found Zaccheus in the tree. So ardent and tireless was his love for the straying that one of the nicknames flung at him by his enemies was "friend of publicans and sinners," or in other words—"friend of lost sheep."

All rescue work is strictly pastoral work. Whenever a minister puts forth an effort to reclaim a member of his church who has wandered away, he is doing a shepherd's work. Some ministers do not mirror this trait of the good shepherd—the disposition to seek the lost; they are interested in the sheep *in* the fold; the sheep outside do not much concern them. They soliloquize thus: "Why do they not come in? If they are outside it is their own fault. The church is open. The Word of God is preached. The sacraments are administered. This is enough." That is a style of argument that brings relief to a certain type of ministerial mind. Such ministers have few converts. The number of accessions on confession is small, but this does not disturb them, for they do not feel any special call to the straying sheep of the house of Israel. They like sheep who do *not* stray; they are fond of good sheep who behave well and give the shepherd no trouble by getting lost. It is a great bother to go after a sheep that has broken away—a sacrifice which it is hardly necessary to make.

There are other ministers who do have a passion for the lost, but only the lost of one particular type, men and women who have never belonged to the church. How to reach the so-called unchurched masses is to these ministers the only great problem. All sorts of devices are adopted to catch them. When any of them are won, that ends the interest of the minister in them. They are now church members, and the work must go forward of rescuing others who are lost. But alas, many of those who have been found soon wander away. They do not remain active in the faith. They are ignorant and foolish and, like sheep, stray from the fold, but the minister does not go after them; he likes sheep lost openly and notoriously, but not straying sheep. He feels incensed that his straying members have forsaken him; he takes it as a personal affront; he resents their habit of roving. He may, in a fit of petulance, say he is glad they are gone. At first they dropped out of the prayer meeting, but he did not go after them, or send anyone else after them. They came only occasionally to the Sunday service, and later on they came not at all, but he gave them no admonition. He was nettled by such backsliding, but said nothing. His sermons, he knows, have been up to high-water mark. The Word of God has been faithfully preached. He has never been more faithful in his study, so that there can be no shortcoming in him. If sheep ramble off, it is because of their own folly; if they straggle behind, it is because they are not worth saving. Many a minister comforts himself in this way. The result is that the losses of the church are tremendous.

Some churches receive large accessions, but never grow. They are always adding new names, but doing nothing greater for the kingdom of God. Every church is losing constantly, and part of the loss is inevitable. Christ lost one of his twelve sheep, and no minister is blameworthy because he does not keep all. But much of the loss is culpable. It could be reduced greatly by more faithful shepherding. Straying sheep could in many cases be brought back if only the shepherd would go after them. Sheep lost for the seventh time could be recovered if someone in the parish possessed the patience and ingenuity of the seeking heart.

Losses to the flock are usually gradual and consequently unnoted. If the minister were to hear some morning that twenty-four of his members were never coming to church again, he would be rightfully alarmed. "Why is this?" he would say. "What is the matter? What is wrong with me or the church that all these people are going away? What sort of wolf or jackal has gotten loose in my flock, causing this demoralization?" But if these church members drop out one at a time, silently and without public notice, one on the average each month, the minister, if not a shepherd, will pay no attention to the drain, even though at the end of two years all the twenty-four will have gone, and the loss to the church will be as great as though all the twenty-four had departed on the same day. The minister who allows one sheep to drop out of his flock without a wound in his heart and without lifting a hand to bring that sheep back is not a good shepherd. A good shepherd dog will wheel round and round the flock, carefully bringing into place every sheep that shows a disposition to lag behind. His instinct tells him that the art of shepherding is the art of taking care of the sheep which is slipping away. He knows in his own brute way that he brings disgrace on the race of shepherd dogs unless he can rescue the sheep that is losing itself. Ought not a shepherd *man* be as wise as a shepherd *dog*?

A minister may be a good sermonizer, he may preside at weddings with grace, and officiate at funerals with dignity; but he is not a good pastor if he maintains an unruffled mind when a solitary member of his flock wanders away. The work of watching demands vigilance, the work of guarding demands prudence, the work of guiding calls for courage, the work of healing involves skill, but the work of rescuing is a work of love. Many a minister would be a better shepherd if he had a more loving heart.

VI. That the feeding of the sheep is an essential duty of the shepherd-calling is known even to those who are least familiar with shepherds and their work. Sheep cannot feed themselves, nor water themselves. They must be conducted to the water and the pasture. The water in Asia is often gotten out of wells, and drawing it is a part of the shepherd's work. The grass varies with the seasons, and the shepherd is ever changing the location of his flock. He shifts it from place to place, keeping it now in the valley and now on the plain, and now leading it to the very mountain top in order that it may be nourished. Everything depends on the proper feeding of the sheep. Unless wisely fed they become emaciated and sick, and the wealth invested in them is squandered. When Ezekiel presents a picture of the bad shepherd, the first stroke of his brush is— "he does not feed the flock." When Jesus hands over the church to Simon Peter, his first word is— "feed." The work of feeding is never to be neglected.

That God feeds his people like a shepherd was an idea full of comfort to the Hebrew heart. He prepares the table; he causes the cup to run over—that is a part of his gracious ministry to men. Jesus claims to be the Good Shepherd, and one of the grounds of his claim is that he feeds. We are to come to him both to drink and to eat. He is the Bread of Life and also the Water of Life.

The idea of feeding is woven into the popular conception of the minister's work. "He does not feed his people" is considered to be among the most damning of accusations which can be brought against the pastor of a church. An English poet has sketched in a single line the portrait of a minister who is not what a minister ought to be: "The hungry sheep look up and are not fed."

But while it is universally admitted that the minister must feed his people, it is surprising how little attention is paid by many a minister to the subject of nutrition and how little thought is given to the art of feeding. Much emphasis has been placed on the art of sermon writing: how to choose the text, how to unfold the idea, how to illustrate and adorn the truth, and how to per-

fect the argument. The world is hardly able to
contain the books which have been written to tell
ministers how to write sermons. But in many of
these books the idea of feeding is not considered.
The sermon is not looked upon as a form of food
to be adapted to a particular appetite and to be
made capable of assimilation by a particular
stomach.

The feeding of a congregation is one of the most
momentous and difficult enterprises which any
man can undertake. There is in every church a
wide variety of ages, temperaments, appetites,
tastes and constitutions, and a great variety of
foods prepared in different ways is consequently
demanded. The lambs are to be fed. Lambs are
of different ages and have differing needs. The
sheep are to be fed. The sheep are of different
grades and natures. The problem of problems is
how to feed all these different kinds of lambs and
sheep on food which shall be suitable for each
one. The pastoral instinct is nowhere more sorely
needed than in the work of preaching.

Many would not call preaching pastoral work
at all, but what is it if it is not pastoral? No part
of a minister's work is more strictly and genu-
inely pastoral than the work of preaching. When
the minister goes into the pulpit, he is the shepherd in the act of feeding, and if every minister
had borne this in mind many a sermon would
have been other than it has been. The curse of
the pulpit is the superstition that a sermon is a

work of art and not a piece of bread or meat. It is
supposed to be a declamation or an oration or a
learned dissertation, something elegant and fine
to be admired and applauded and talked about
by eulogizing saints, or carped at by stiff-necked,
unreasonable sinners. Sermons, rightly understood, are primarily forms of food. They are articles of diet. They are meals served by the minister for the sustenance of spiritual life. If this
could be remembered it would help many a minister to get rid of his stilted language and to cut
off a lot of his rhetorical ruffles; it would free him
from his bombastic elocution and burn up his or-
namental introductions and skyrocket perora-
tions.

The shepherd's work is plain and humble.
What true shepherd ever tried to make a show?
A shepherd has his eyes upon the sheep, and his
first concern is that the sheep shall have enough
to eat. Feeding sheep is not romantic; the poetic
element in it is not conspicuous. It is not an act
which can be done with a flourish. It is prosaic
but vital work, and is never well done unless it is
done by a man who has an honest and an earnest
heart.

There are few preachers who preach simply
enough. Their language is too bookish and
their style is too involved. They want to be
Demosthenes or Cicero and are not content to be
a shepherd. An interesting book could be written on pastoral preaching, preaching that indi-

vidualizes and feeds. How to make sermons that will pass easily into the blood, how to unfold Bible texts in a way that will furnish nutriment to the nerves of feeling and action, how to offer truth so as to satisfy the cravings of the human heart and make it strong in the doing of God's will—is not that one of the cardinal problems of the minister? And has it been, do you think, sufficiently considered?

Pastoral work is not simply making social calls; pastoral work is also preaching. The minister does not cease to be a pastor when he goes into the pulpit; he then takes up one of the shepherd's most exacting and serious tasks. We sometimes hear it said of a minister: "He is a good pastor, but he cannot preach." The sentence is self-contradictory. No man can be a good pastor who cannot preach, any more than a man can be a good shepherd and still fail to feed his flock. A part of shepherding is feeding, and an indispensable part. Some of the finest and most effective of all a minister's pastoral work is done in his sermon. In a sermon he can warn, protect, guide, heal, rescue, and nourish. The shepherd in him comes to lofty stature in the pulpit.

It is well for a minister to ask himself now and then: "Am I a good pastor in the pulpit? Or am I keeping the people too long in one particular field because I happen to like the landscape from that standpoint? Am I compelling them to browse too long in my favorite pasture? Have they nibbled every green thing in it down to the earth, and are they hungry now for grass that grows higher up on the mountain? When I preach, am I doing a shepherd's work? Am I feeding the lambs or am I elevating myself? Am I playing with words or am I breaking bread? Am I building beautiful pyramids or am I drawing water? Am I soaring like an eagle or am I satisfying hunger? Am I a hireling, preaching for applause, or am I a herder and feeder of souls?" There is nothing which will so chasten a minister in his sermonic preparation and so discipline his style as facing the shepherd idea. Christ was the great teacher, and because he was the great teacher he was also the Good Shepherd. A shepherd who is skilled in his work never fails to feed his flock.

VII. The Oriental shepherd did one thing more—he loved the sheep. He loved them in a way unknown to Occidental shepherds. His relations to them were closer and more tender than anything found in the modern sheep-raising world. The solitude of those Eastern lands created wondrous intimacies between animal and human life. Man and beast became linked together by ties beautiful and sacred. There sprang up in the sheep a fondness for the shepherd, and in the shepherd an affection for the sheep, which were displayed in many ways. Here is a lovely touch: "He calleth his own sheep by name." It was not necessary that he should give to each sheep a name, but he did it because he liked them.

Love always individualizes. It takes delight in coining pet names. It is not love if it is not personal and intimate. Here is another touch: "He carries the lambs in his bosom." It was not necessary that he do this, but he did it because he liked them. When the shepherd was not watching or guarding or guiding or healing or saving or feeding, he was doing something finer than any of these—he was communing with the sheep, playing with them, talking to them, and entering so far as a man could into their poor brute life. The result was that the sheep were devoted to the shepherd. They knew his voice; every cadence of it was music, every inflection was an inspiration. The shepherd was a lover of the sheep, and it was because of his attachment to them that in time of danger he thought not of himself, but of them. In defending them he was willing to lay down his life. This was the crowning virtue of the shepherd—his self-sacrificing love.

It is also the crowning excellence of all the shepherds of Christ's sheep. Paul says to the Colossians: "Above all these things put on love, which is the bond of perfectness." Paul is thinking of the soul as being clothed with the Christian virtues. Around these various beautiful manifestations of the Christian spirit must be thrown the greatest of the virtues—love. Whatever other virtues a shepherd of Christ's sheep may have, without love he is poor and naked. He must have many virtues, but the one that gives vitality to all of them, and which binds them all together, is love. He has various works to do, but his supreme work is loving. If he loves he will do all the things which shepherds ought to do. He will watch! When did love ever have drowsy eyelids? Love can outrun the longest night. He will guard! Love shields with jealous care. Love protects at all hazards. He will guide! Love has far-seeing eyes. Love detects the pitfalls and finds safe paths into the land of peace. He will heal! The hands of love are gentle. Love binds up wounds. He will seek and save! Love cannot sleep so long as the one it loves is on the mountain in the storm. He will feed! Love is the great nourisher at life's feast. Love satisfies.

Would you know, then, the work of a shepherd? Look at Jesus of Nazareth, that great Shepherd of the sheep, who stands before us forever the perfect pattern of shepherdhood, the flawless example for all who are entrusted with the care of souls. "I am the Good Pastor," he says, "I watch, I guard, I guide, I heal, I rescue, I feed. I love from the beginning, and I love to the end. Follow me!"

3

THe
SHepHerd's OppoRTuNity

You have all heard that the day of the preacher is gone. The printing press has taken away his occupation. He still goes on speaking, but it is to a dwindling congregation, and by and by all the pews may be empty. The decadence of the pulpit is one of the popular themes of our day. The contrast between the modern pulpit pygmy and the pulpit giant of a former age is a subject with which sportive spirits make merry.

And now it is beginning to be whispered that the day of the *pastor* also is gone. The modern world has no need of a shepherd. The typical pastor of bygone generations is an antiquated figure for whom no room can be found on the stage of our modern world. The ancient custom of catechizing children from house to house, and calling entire households together for Bible reading and prayer, the fatherly offices of counsel and admonition, and the gracious and intimate ministry of the spiritual guide—all this is a fashion which has passed away. The world has outgrown the need of a shepherd. Education has fitted men to think and act for themselves. Man is no longer a sheep. Every man is his own shepherd. Pastoral guidance is an impertinence. Wealth has increased and has brought with it a new sense of self-confidence and independence which will not brook interference from an ecclesiastical official. Men now have many helps which they did not possess in former days. A multitude of magazines and books furnish all the information and stimulus which are needed. The pastor knows nothing which it is not possible for the alert layman to know. He may, like other men, make social calls and chat about things of current interest, but the old need for pastoral attention is gone. Whatever guidance is desired will be gotten from leaders who speak in printer's ink.

Besides all this, men are living in strenuous days and have no time to be talked to by a pastor. Business is business and cannot be dropped even for a moment in the heat of the day. Multitudes leave home for their work in the early morning and return fagged at evening time. Through a larger part of the day the children are at school, and during the afternoon the women are absorbed in their social functions. There is ordinarily no hour in the day in which a pastor can meet the entire household. There is no eager anticipation, therefore, of the coming of the pastor. He is busy, and so is everyone else; pastoral service, being largely uncalled for and consequently perfunctory, can be dispensed with without loss.

In large cities the difficulties are especially great. There is no parish system among our Protestant churches and members of each congregation are scattered over wide areas, rendering pastoral visitation so laborious that church members in large numbers cease to demand it of their minister. Moreover, a considerable section of society has become nomadic in its habits. Men and women flit south in the winter and north in the summer and across the oceans between times, and occasionally make a tour of the world. Thousands of Christians own summer homes in which they live the larger part of the year. The winter months in the city are so crowded that pastoral attention seems an imposition. Modern civilization has escorted the pastor to the front door and politely bowed him out.

Such is the conclusion of many, but it is mistaken. The age of the shepherd has just arrived. Never has he been so much needed as now. Never before have there been so many important things for him to do. To be sure, he cannot do his work in the old way. The old order ever changes. New occasions teach new duties, and time makes ancient forms of doing things uncouth. The pastor of the early days in his special clothes is no longer in demand, but the world awaits a shepherd who can meet the needs of the present hour.

In one sense the world is always changing, and in another sense it is evermore the same. Steam and electricity alter many things; other things they do not touch. They have not changed the processes of the growth of a grain of corn, nor have they modified the appetites and passions of the human heart. The soul is now what it has been from the beginning, and now as always it needs a shepherd's care. Civilization transforms the surface; the interior life it leaves untouched.

Schools and colleges do not make obsolete a shepherd's work. The young men now coming from our universities are as much in need of pastoral guidance as any men in the world. Thousands of them are confused in their religious thinking, not able yet to reconcile the teachings of Christ with what they have learned from their professors. The traditional faith is no longer tenable, and they have not gained another to take its place. Does anybody suppose that a college diploma renders a man immune to all diseases, so that he is no longer in need of a physician? Why should it be imagined that a college course lifts a man above the need of the healing power of a physician sent by the Son of God?

That which education cannot do is also beyond the power of money. Money may render men lofty-minded and harden their hearts to the influences of a spiritual adviser, but the needs of a rich man are as great as those of his poorest brother. Does not our Lord say that it is hard for a rich man to enter into the kingdom of God? If this be true, the rich man is in special need of assistance, and who is better fitted to give him aid than the shepherd? Rich people are more like poor people than is sometimes conceded. Both alike are exposed to temptations, and both alike suffer disappointment and sorrow. Into the homes of the rich and the poor sickness comes, and death, and the desolation of bereavement, and the darkness of doubt and despair. Rich men, with their hands filled with gold, can lose the higher treasures of faith and hope and love, and, though living in fine houses, they can be miserable and poor and blind and naked. It is a great mistake to assume that well-to-do people have no need of a shepherd.

The minister who neglects or scorns the rich is unworthy of his calling. It is a popular delusion that pastors are always inclined to devote more time to the rich man than to the poor, whereas the fact is that poor people are not nearly so likely to be neglected by the average pastor as the rich. Not so many rich people would have lost their early faith and degenerated into social idlers and conscienceless worldlings if they had received more continuous and faithful pastoral care. There is no class more neglected in our great cities than the rich.

The pastoral work in a rich community is far more difficult than in a community which is poor. It was easier for Christ to help a poor man than a rich man, and that has been the experience of all his ministers. But the rich men in Christ's day always had his sympathy and attention and to them full offers of his grace were given. The poorest beggar and the richest publican in Jericho were alike the recipients of his bounty.

Money is never going to take away the occupation of the shepherd, nor will the printing press crowd him out. Instead of books dispensing with the shepherd's labor, they give him infinitely more to do. It is printed matter which causes a lot of mischief in our modern world. Many false prophets have gone abroad, and they wear books' clothing. All sorts of wolves and jackals, of serpents also and birds of prey, are moving through the world scattering and tearing the sheep. The literature of unbelief is enormous, and millions are reading it. Fools and dunces, ignoramuses and fanatics, knaves and mischief-makers of many stripes, are writing for the daily papers and magazines, and pour forth in books their shallow thoughts and low ideals and pestilential fancies upon the world. Anybody, no matter how stupid in mind and corrupt in heart, can write a book and find a multitude to read it. False notions, half truths, shallow reasonings, wild vagaries, crazy hallucinations, pretentious philosophizings, silly prophecies and darkening interpretations sweep over the world like a flood. Immature and diseased and ill-formed and half-baked minds utilize the printing press in disseminating schemes and programs which if adopted would upset the world. Never has there been such need for sound brains and sane thinking. Never has there been so loud a call for shepherds fitted by natural endowment and training to lead men out of the morasses of erroneous opinions into the hill country of Christian truth.

One who comes into close touch with individual men is amazed often at the perverted notions and curious misinterpretations of Christianity which sometimes lodge in the heads of apparently intelligent men. Even persons who have attended church services for years sometimes betray the most astonishing ignorance in regard to things one would have supposed they had mastered in childhood. In thousands of cases, teaching from the pulpit does not reach the special need of the individual mind. It is only by talking face to face with one person, as Christ talked face to face with Nicodemus, and face to face with the woman at the well, that the root of the difficulty is reached and the darkness is scattered. The printing press has created new kingdoms for the shepherd to conquer.

It is true that the pastoral problem in great cities is peculiarly intricate and baffling, but no one who knows the modern city would deny that the city needs the shepherd. It is here that the crowds make one think of the crowds which reminded Jesus of sheep scattered and without a shepherd. It is the tragedy of the city that such multitudes have no one to care for them. Thousands of young men are there without parents, and with no strong friend to give counsel. Thousands of girls are there without a mother, and with no one to take a mother's place. Thousands of men and women in middle life are there, broken in health and also in hope, who have surrendered the ideals of their early years. The aged are there, looking wistfully at the western sky and wondering. Difficult it is indeed to shepherd so great a multitude, but because a task is difficult is no reason why it should be abandoned. After the pessimist has painted the picture of a city situation as black as he can paint it, and has put into it every difficulty and obstacle to pastoral service which his eye has seen or his mind has conceived, the true minister of Christ will not be daunted but will plunge at once, bold-hearted, into pastoral work. It is a work which requires extraordinary wisdom, unfailing patience, plodding fidelity, unfaltering boldness, a genius for hope, abiding faith, and boundless love; but there is none other that is more clearly the work that Christ just now wishes done, and upon the faithful performance of which the future of humanity more manifestly depends. The cities must be saved, and they are to be saved by shepherds.

It must be conceded that a pastor does not have as good a chance to shine as formerly. There was a patriarchal dignity and splendor belonging to the shepherd of the earlier time which can never be reproduced. Our modern shepherd cannot be so conspicuous. He cannot stand upon a pedestal. He cannot be so picturesque. But he can still be useful, and this, after all, is in Jesus' thought the highest honor within the reach of mortals. The modern shepherd can be leaven. He can be salt. He can be light. He can go about doing good. He can give. He can be the servant of all. He can lay down his life. The God who is building the world of our day has left in it a large and glorious place for the shepherd.

Let us measure the dimensions of the opportunity for pastoral service which is now presented. Note, first of all, how sorely our churches need it. For years we have been hearing constantly of decreasing church attendance and reduced accessions, and of lowered Sunday school membership, not in one quarter but in many quarters of the Christian world. There are those who feel that the church has come to a crisis, and men are asking if Jesus is indeed the one who was expected or whether it is time to begin to look for another. Along with this shrinking of numbers in our churches and Bible schools and schools of theology, there has gone on a continual shortening of the pastorate. Ministers do not stay with their churches as they used to stay. After a year or two or three, both minister and people are too often glad to sever the pastoral relation. The pastor departs for pastures new, a fresh committee is appointed, and the ordeal of finding the ideal man is once more gone through with. Sometimes, however, the minister stays, to the consternation of many hearts. The peace of the parish is not what it ought to be, there is discontent in the heart of the minister and dissatisfaction in the hearts of the people. Never, perhaps, have there been so many restless and faultfinding churches as within recent years.

Varied efforts have been made to deal with the situation. Different physicians have made divers diagnoses, and the remedies prescribed have been diverse. One man has said: "Let us enrich the service; people do not come to church because the worship is thin and bald. Let us borrow miscellaneous bits of ritual and adorn the order of our service; thus will the church make herself attractive to many who have hitherto stayed away." Another has said: "Let us revise our creed. It is too long and too scholastic. Men of our day are offended by doctrines couched in the language of the past. Let us write a shorter creed. Or, since many men are skeptical in regard to what were once called fundamentals, let us do away with creeds altogether. Thus will be made a wide-open door and multitudes will enter." Another has said: "Let us advertise our services. Let us tell the town what we are doing. Advertising is legitimate; let us use the newspapers and flood the town with invitation cards; let us blazon abroad the fact that all are welcome. Thus will men know that things are moving and that the church is interested in their souls." Still another has said: "Let us organize the men; let us band them together in leagues and clubs. Our men hitherto have done but little; let us get them interested in missions and in various forms of church activity, and then the kingdom of God will come with power." Another has suggested: "Let us send for an evangelist, a man who has a genius for catching the public ear. What is needed is a prophet with flaming tongue who can draw and hold the people, forcing them to a decision for Christ and the church. Let us organize mass meetings, with a great and glorious choir, and by the sheer attractiveness of the program let us compel the unwilling to come in." Another has said: "We can do nothing with our present preacher—he is a good man, but he cannot preach. He means well, but his tongue is tedious. He is not great enough for so exceptional a field. He might do well where the people are less cultured, but for a congregation so critical and fastidious a different type of man is a necessity."

All these six doctors have agreed in this, that the one thing essential is an attraction strong enough to draw men inside a consecrated building. Their common assumption has been that the work of Christ is really prosperous only when crowds are assembled in his name, and that the supreme problem of the Christian church is how to devise a Sunday service so attractive that people cannot stay away. And so in many a field one or two or more of these six expedients have been tried. The service has been enriched and then made still richer. The creed has been whittled down until nothing at all remained. The advertisements have been large and vivid, and printer's ink has flowed in rivers. The men have been organized and reorganized, and drilled in the art of holding dinners at which only expert speakers gave eloquent advice. Evangelists of vast prestige have delivered their stirring message, and then hurried on their flaming way. One minister has been succeeded by another, in the hope that Chrysostom the golden-mouthed might finally appear. But alas, after all the remedies have been tested, the last state of the church has, in many instances, been worse than the first. It is a stiff-necked generation with which the church today has to deal, and these promising experimentations seem impotent in bringing it to Christ.

Now and then someone has ventured to suggest that the church should go to the people instead of the people coming to the church, and the new idea has been carried out for a month or two with enthusiasm and high hope. The minister has locked up his church and gone into a theater or into a tent or out upon the street corner, bringing his message to all who would hear. In this enterprising mission some of the faithful have accompanied him, glad to prove by the crucifixion of their tastes and inclinations that they were

sincerely desirous of doing the work of the Lord.
But in spite of all these efforts, prosperity has lin-
gered, and churches by the score have felt themselves discomfited and conquered. After a spasm
of zeal the old coolness crept in again. There were
crowds for a season, and then the old empty pews
were as conspicuous as they were at first.

Only here and there has it been recognized that
the solution of the problem lies in the shepherd—
one who goes where the sheep are, not with a
grand declamation, but with a heart that loves
and solaces and heals. He must live with the
people, think with their mind, feel with their
heart, see with their eyes, hear with their ears,
suffer with their spirit. He must bear their griefs
and carry their sorrows. He must be wounded
for their transgressions and bruised for their in-
iquities. The chastisement of their peace must be
upon him, and with his stripes they must be
healed. They all like sheep have gone astray, and
he must be willing to have laid on him the iniquity of them all. It is the sacrificial note in the
ministry which is too often lacking in these latter
days. The minister has become too much a man
of a book. Like the ancient scribes, he is a scholar
and sometimes a pedant.

When the Good Shepherd appeared in Galilee, the contrast between him and the other shepherds was perceived at once. There was a sympathy in Jesus' tone and a gentleness in his touch
which proved at once that he was with the people

in their sorrows and upward strivings. The chief
trouble with the modern church is that in too
many localities it has lost contact with the life of
the town. It is out of touch with the souls of men
in their present perplexities and needs, and hence
it cannot influence them. The impression is
abroad that Christianity is a pretty speech, a bit
of idealism, a lovely dream, a stanza of poetry, a
piece of Sunday acting, something that the
preacher can say by rote, and to which the saints
can say, "Amen"—and not a sober, serious, week-
day life. What the world most wants today is
shepherding. The world has many comforts,
luxuries in abundance; what it lacks is love. Love
cannot be satisfactorily expressed to our generation in printer's ink, in evangelistic appeals, in
pulpit eloquence, or in doctrinal statements. The
expression which the world now demands is the
love of the shepherd who takes the lambs in his
bosom, who gently leads those who have their
young, and who day by day lays down his life
for the sheep. A generation ago the Word of God
was the Bible; today the Word of God must be
Jesus and the man who has the spirit of Jesus. A
genuine Christian is the only epistle which the
world now cares to read. Multitudes care little
for worship, less for church polity, still less for
creeds, nothing for traditions and ceremonies.
Character is everything. Shepherding work is the
work for which humanity is crying. The twentieth century is the century of the shepherd.

The shortening of pastorates is due to the fact that the tenderness and sacredness of the old pastoral relation are fading out. The relation of the minister to the church is now too often that of a platform speaker to an audience, of a reformer to a community, of an engineer to a machine, and not that of a friend to a company of friends. If the minister is simply a Sunday lecturer, he can leave town any day and no one will be sadder. If he is only a public reformer, he can depart at the end of any week and many persons will be glad. If he is a machinist, expert in managing organizations, his place can easily be filled by another—engineers are abundant. If he is a shepherd, if he knows his sheep by name, and if his sheep know his voice, he cannot pass from one fold to another without a great loneliness and heaviness of spirit, and without deep wounds in the hearts of those he leaves behind him. It is because the shepherd idea is faint and the orator or preacher idea is so largely dominant that churches are able to change ministers with such slight concern, and that ministers can pass from one parish to another with lightness of heart and even rejoicing. If the Church of Christ is to be saved, she must be born again into the glory of the shepherd idea.

That a multitude today need shepherding cannot be disputed. The present moral and religious situation is too well known to demand description here. It has been photographed again and again and printed in colors, and the pictures have been held before our eyes so that there is no excuse for confused notions as to the present condition of mankind. It is a somber world on which the electric lights of our brilliant civilization fall. When Jesus looked upon the crowds in Galilee, he at once thought of a neglected flock of sheep. The shepherds of Palestine had not done their duty. The plight of the people was pitiable. Matthew says that Jesus was moved with compassion because the people were like sheep, distressed and scattered. The description is graphic. By "distressed" one is to understand "worried, harassed, vexed, tired out, exhausted." In the other word, "scattered," we have a picture of a lot of sheep thrown down, one or two lying in this place, a few in that place, still another group in a third place. The unity of the flock is broken because of the attacks of enemies and the lack of a shepherd's care.

What two better words can be found to paint the present situation? Are not multitudes today distressed in body, mind, and estate? It is an age of reconstruction, reorganization, readjustment. Mighty movements are taking place in the industrial and commercial worlds. Conditions fluctuate, work is unsteady, positions are insecure. Money takes wings and flies away. Even giants are pushed unmercifully to the wall. It is a money-making age, and men are harassed by the care of wealth. Great fortunes bring with them multiplied anxieties, and the sight of colossal wealth breeds in many minds sour envy and fevered discontent. It is an age of machinery. Steel and electricity perform a lot of work, but never have men been more weary and more heavy-laden than just now. Multitudes are perplexed in regard to the things of the Spirit. It is an age of new ideas, novel interpretations, bold hypotheses, daring innovations. Everything is the object of furious assault. The industry of the printing press, by giving voice to the thoughts and imaginings of a multitude of minds, has converted the earth into a tower of Babel, and men are living in a welter of confusion. Intellectual difficulties and practical perplexities combine to cause the present distress. What shall I think? What shall I believe? Which way shall I go? What shall I do? What is true? What is right? What is duty?—in this strange, complex, discordant, bewildered twentieth century. Surely the world today is calling loudly for guidance. The distress of the multitude is a cry in the ears of the Church of God for shepherds.

Men are distressed and they are scattered. Irresistible forces have driven them apart. Millions have passed from one country into another. In our larger cities live great numbers of men and women who were born in foreign lands. Other millions have passed from rural life into cities. The old homes are broken up, the old ties are severed, families are scattered. Industrial forces drive men into separated groups and classes. The wage earner and the capitalist have never been farther apart. People are classified according to their financial resources. Every city has its elegant avenues and its grimy slums. Men are segregated by forces over which they have no control. There are chasms as deep and bridgeless as the gulf in the parable of Dives and Lazarus. The result is an enormous mass of suspicion and envy and ill-will. Large sections of society are sour. The disgruntled are numbered by the tens of thousands. If hate is murder, then the world today is in a murderous mood. There are quarters in which the Church can do no mighty works because of these social estrangements. There are other quarters in which the message of the Church is not even listened to, so stubborn is the prejudice and so bitter the resentment. What humanity just now needs is a great host of peacemakers, men who shall serve as mediators between hostile classes of society. What is needed is the persuasive tone, the gentle approach, the sympathetic touch. It is the shepherd rather than the herald who is needed now, not the man who can deliver eloquent proclamations but the man who goes about doing good.

It is easy to criticize a sermon, it is not so easy to scoff at goodwill manifested in lovely ways. The man who tears the creed to shreds will succumb to repeated acts of kindness. Even the skeptic who is fond of saying that all Christians are hypocrites and all preachers hirelings, cannot permanently stand up against the pressure of a loving heart. The impression prevalent in the non-churchgoing world is that ministers are talkers, salaried palaverers paid to say sweet and soothing things for the men who pay their salaries. There is nothing which will break down this prejudice like the self-sacrificing labors of a shepherd. The questions are often discussed—"How can we reach the unchurched masses—how can we gain the wage earner—how can we win the laboring man?" It is safe to say the orator will not win him, nor will the theologian, nor the doctor of philosophy, nor the connoisseur in literature. He will surrender only to the shepherd.

Ezekiel in his description of the religious condition of his day adds a touch which is not expressed in the two adjectives "distressed" and "scattered." After dwelling on the fact that sheep in his day were scattered, the prophet then adds, "They became food to all the beasts of the field." The description of that far-off day is true also to present fact. In all times of skepticism and confusion, men become the easy victims of charlatans and fanatics. Those who wander away from Christianity and feed themselves on husks, by and by become so hungry that they throw themselves into the arms of the first pretentious religious leader who happens to cross their path. Nothing is more amazing than the credulity of those who have found Christianity too hard to accept. There is no page of recent history more saddening than the story of the rise and prosperity of a multitude of religious movements which must inevitably at last come to nothing. The United States, proudest of all countries of her churches and schools, is a paradise for religious impostors and magicians. This is because of our worldliness and the practical godlessness of large classes of our well-to-do people. The type of man represented in the New Testament by Simon the Sorcerer has never become extinct, and in enlightened America, as in benighted Samaria, whenever Simon (or his wife) appears and gives out that he himself is some great one, many give heed from the least to the greatest, saying: "This man is that power of God which is called great." Every large city swarms with cults whose devotees are fed on various philosophical concoctions more or less tinctured with the Christian flavor. And the wolves are as shrewd as ever—they fatten on the sheep. Men and women are as helpless as of old. Unless shepherded, they become "food to all the beasts of the field."

Ezekiel represents God as mourning over the situation. "My sheep wandered through all the mountains and upon every high hill. Yea, my sheep were scattered upon all the face of the earth, and there was none that did search or seek after them." The situation is not as dark as it was then. Thousands of faithful shepherds are in the field. But the number is not sufficient for the present crisis.

The individual is slipping out of sight. Many things conspire to submerge him. By the steam engine, factories and mills were created, and men were summoned from their homes and small shops to work in groups in huge buildings. In that day they ceased to be individuals and degenerated into "hands." The principle of cooperation in the business world has worked itself out in corporations, syndicates and trusts, the individual disappearing in this larger person created by the State. The growth of cities has a tendency to obliterate the outlines of individuality, and men when massed together forget their individual worth. "What matters it what I think or say or do here in this great city?" Such is the soliloquy which rises spontaneously to many lips.

The emphasis of modern thought on heredity and environment as controlling influences on human life has also worked to break down in multitudes the sense of personal accountability. Children are not to blame since they are what they are because of their parents; and their parents are not to blame because they are the products of society. In this way the individual conscience is dulled and the flame of personal responsibility is snuffed out. The talk today is about the social problem, the corporate responsibility, the institutional function. Society looms large and the individual man dwindles. Here is a call for the shepherd. The shepherd has an individualizing eye. He sees the solitary sheep. He cares for the personal need. The good shepherd always says: "I know my own, and my own know me." He calls his own sheep by name.

It is an interesting fact that the last sentence which we can trace to the pen of St. John is: "Salute the friends by name." John is the man who came nearest to the Good Shepherd's heart, and who narrated in his Gospel the allegory in which Jesus says that the Shepherd calls his own sheep by name; and the last time John speaks to us he tells us not to forget this personal and individualizing touch.

All the apostles are great teachers of individualism. They learned it from the Master. One of the most thrilling chapters in the New Testament is the last chapter of Paul's letter to the Romans. It is a list of names which ought to be read often in our churches. The names mean nothing to us, but they meant everything to the men and women who owned them, and it ought to warm our hearts to think how warm their hearts became when that chapter was read before the congregation. We think of Paul as a matchless theologian; we do not think of him often enough as an ideal pastor. He was a faithful shepherd even to death. In the Roman prison, condemned to die, writing his last letter, he closes with a paragraph which is beautifully pastoral: "Salute Prisca and Aquila, and the house of Onesiphorus. Erastus remained at Corinth; but Trophimus I left at Miletus sick." Strange, is it not, that the last letter of the greatest of the apostles should end with matters so tame and insignificant? It is *not* strange. The manner of the ending of Paul's last letter and the style of the ending of John's last letter is a revelation—it reveals the place in the Christian church of the shepherd's touch.

It is worth noting that Matthew couples the compassion of our Lord over the sheep that are distressed and scattered with the exhortation: "Pray the Lord of the harvest that he send forth laborers into his harvest." There is enormous pastoral work to do today, and the shepherds are few. It is one of your duties to keep praying, and to teach your people to pray that more laborers may go forth to the work. If this is your prayer and also the prayer of the people, you will by and by have a corps of volunteer pastors, trained and directed by yourself in the doing of pastoral service. So when your church becomes a larger one, you can readily have in addition one or more salaried co-shepherds, in order that every form of pastoral service may be promptly and faithfully attended to. If your church is in a great city, you already need a staff of pastors, for in proportion to the effectiveness of the pastoral ministration will your church meet the needs of the situation and accomplish the work which God at this time desires to make prosper in your hands.

•　　　•　　　•

Two ideas are in the air which are influencing

many minds: efficiency and conservation. One reads these two words on every hand. They have worked their way into common conversation. Everywhere men are asking, How can I be more efficient? and How can I save that which is now going to waste? Businessmen are overhauling their systems, trying to see at what point they can make improvement. The intensity of competition makes it necessary that all bungling and wasteful methods be gotten rid of. Every part of the business must be brought up to the highest pitch of perfection. Men are looking for results. The machinery must produce as large a product as possible. The ratio between the energy put in and the resulting product must be improved. Fortune hangs upon this. The continued existence of the business depends on it. The standards are everywhere going up. What was counted good enough ten years ago is not tolerated now. Every capable businessman is demanding a higher grade of efficiency in every department of his business.

In the realm of agriculture this aspiration has already worked astonishing results. All over the world men are at work on the problem of how to increase the yield of the soil. It is now quite certain that we have only begun to get out of the soil what the soil is ready to give, and that all the dismal prophecies of the population outstripping the power of the soil to sustain it are figments of the ignorant imagination. A wise man has recently remarked, "We must get down to the ground if we want to get the most out of it." This is equally true of the minister; if he would get the most out of the people he must come down to where they are. The church is like a farm. The average church does not yield as much as it should. Men are rightfully demanding of the church greater harvests. They assert it does not do enough for social betterment. Considering its numbers, its wealth and its culture, the church is not measuring up to present-day expectations. Ministers, as well as farmers, must set themselves to a restudy of the soil. The "yield" can be doubled and quadrupled with wider knowledge and more abundant skill.

One of the several steps needed is a restudy of human nature. This would result in a more painstaking care for the individual life. We minsters have been too much in the clouds. There have been too many generalities, too much reliance on wholesale methods, too much slapdash, hit-or-miss, helter-skelter action to produce satisfactory results. If farmers can add a stalk to the number of stalks growing in every hill of corn, why should not ministers increase by pain and prayer the number of saints now growing in their church? If farmers can add, by taking thought, three ounces to the weight of the average ear of corn, ministers might possibly increase, by obedience to the laws of God, the weight of Christian character in the average member of their congregations. "Too few new converts, too many light and dwarfed Christians"—is not this the accusation that might fairly be written on the wall of many a church? The work that pastors do in these rigorous, exacting days must be finer and closer, more intelligent and scientific, more faithful and painstaking, more personal and delicate, than has been much of the work in the past. Shepherding work—knowing every sheep by name, giving every sheep a chance to know the shepherd—this is the direction in which an awakened church is bound to move.

The other idea, conservation, has risen to prominence because of the passion for efficiency. It is because men are severely practical and demand larger results that the thought of waste has become unendurable. Economy has become a watchword among the nations of the earth. How can we utilize waste products? How can we bring into service the energy which is now squandered? How can we husband the forces which are going to waste? This is the question which all alert men everywhere are asking. Because the world's population is increasing, a great deal of work must be done. All our resources are needed. We cannot afford to let our treasures go to waste. The nation itself is setting an example to all our people. She is surveying her swamps, and asking how they may be converted into fertile farms. She is measuring her deserts and laying plans to irrigate them. She is computing the value of her forests and taking measures to prevent their destruction. The various nations are estimating the power of their waterfalls and calculating the work which they may do. Men looked with envy on Niagara until they got out of it both power and light. They now look with envy on the tides, and the question today is how to make the oceans work for us, creating our light and our heat. The material resources are being scanned with an economic eye, and are being used with a more thrifty and a more frugal hand.

It is in its treatment of human life, however, that the genius of our age is best exemplified. What a host of experts are working on the problem of feeding and nutrition, health and disease. Human life has been hitherto wasted horribly. Thousands of lives have been sacrificed to the incompetency of governments, tens of thousands to the ignorance of individuals. The world is awakening to the value of life.

It is not God's good pleasure that disease should fill our cemeteries with premature graves. Cities are making war on the death rate. Already it has been reduced amazingly. In great laboratories of research, men are studying food values and are grading articles of diet according to their energy-producing power. They are mastering the art of warding off disease. Prophylaxis, or the art of preventing disease, has come to the front; and a new class of medicines, the prophylactics, have taken precedence over all others. The surgeon's knife was once deadly to an extent which now appalls us, but antiseptics have made the majority of surgical operations safe. Specialists are now at work to discover how to hasten the processes of recuperation and to bring health more swiftly to tissues which have been ravaged by disease. The present age is interested in life, physical life, the life of the body, to a degree never before known. As a result, the length of life is increasing. Men were once old at sixty—multitudes are not old now at seventy. The day is coming when men who obey the laws of God will not be old at eighty. If we cannot add a cubit to our stature, we can at least add a span to our earthly life by knowing how to live.

Here is the pastor's opportunity to gather hints for his own improvement in the art of saving souls. It is not necessary that so much spiritual energy should be wasted; it is not God's will that so many souls should die. Medicine has given us a clue. The modern physician is nothing if not individualistic. Physicians never deal with men in crowds. "One patient at a time"—that is the rule in all hospitals throughout the world. Each patient has his own chart at the head of his bed. The temperature of his body, the beat of his pulse, and the number of his respirations are carefully noted. Each patient has his own diet, his special remedies, and his particular kind of nursing. It is this sleepless vigilance, this jealous guardianship, this minuteness of observation and delicate accuracy of treatment of the individual man which has filled the modern world with miracles and given the physicians of the body their unparalleled prestige. It is not by spectacular and scenic methods that the death rate of great cities is reduced, but by the loving care of the one baby, the faithful nursing of the one patient who without this care and nursing would have died.

The same policy adopted in our churches would bring equally astonishing results. Under our present system vast volumes of energy go to waste. Christian men and women are filled with energy, but in many cases the energy turns no wheels. There is in every church a Niagara of force which creates neither heat nor light. There is in every church desert land which would blossom as a rose if it were irrigated by an engineer's skill. There are swamps which could be drained if only the necessary knowledge and genius were at hand.

There are in every church three classes of people whose life is now running largely to waste. First, the inactive Christians; second, the publicans and sinners; third, the Samaritans. These are the three classes upon which the shepherd must bestow appropriate and constant care. An inactive Christian is, of course, lost—lost so far as God's purposes are concerned. What matters it whether his name is on the church book if he does nothing for the advancement of God's kingdom? The publicans and sinners are apostates, those who have slipped down into open estrangement from the church. The Samaritans are just outside the church, earthy and heretical—and yet in God's plan, Samaria is always a part of the promised land.

The shepherds of the Jewish church before Jesus came had allowed all three classes to slip away from them. Multitudes of Jews were mere formalists, lacking the life of the Spirit; others had become utterly hopeless in the eyes of the shepherds; while Samaria was counted accursed, her people unfit to associate with and her very existence a vexation to the pious Hebrew heart. When the Good Shepherd arrived he understood his business. He at once proceeded to make use of all three classes. He sent idlers into the vineyard. He laid hold of the publicans and sinners, and even of Samaria he said: "Lift up your eyes and look at the fields—they are white already unto the harvest." To him who looks upon the world with Jesus' eyes there are no hopeless deserts, no irreclaimable swamps, nor is there any Samaria which cannot be made a part of the Holy Land. Jesus was master of the method for transforming human nature, and his was the pastoral method. He made his way into the Sanhedrin through the soul of one old man. He touched the hearts of all publicans the day he befriended one of them. And he broke the hard heart of Samaria simply by being kind to one Samaritan woman.

When we see that the work of the Christian

church is work on the *individual,* it is then that no
parish, however limited in territory, seems really
small. There is an unimaginable amount of work
to be done in every church. Young men ought
not to feel that their life is thrown away because
they cannot preach great sermons before a crowd.
Get rid of the oratorical conception of the ministry and put in its place the *pastoral* idea. You ought
not to turn your back upon a church because it
seems dull and dead. What church could have
been more dull, stupid and hopeless than the
valley of the Vosges before Oberlin took hold of
it? What church could have been more irreligious,
reprobate, and godless than Kidderminster before Baxter gave his great heart to it? Never believe that there is a church on the earth, however
desolate or demon-possessed, that cannot be
made to blossom with the flowers of paradise
under the summer warmth created by a
shepherd's care.

4

The
Shepherd's Temptations

The shepherd's temptations are many. Let us look at but two. These two are singled out because they are the two against which our Lord and two of his apostles uttered special and repeated warnings, and because the experience of nineteen hundred years has demonstrated that these two are most insidious, most constant, and most fatal. They are the love of gain and the love of power: covetousness and ambition; inordinate desire to possess for personal gratification and an unlawful love of advancement, prominence, authority. Christian history makes it clear that these are the cardinal sins which ever lie like crouching beasts at the shepherd's door.

Covetousness is often associated in our mind with money, and it seems absurd to say that one of the two besetting sins of the minister is an inordinate love of money. The world is always ready to accuse the minister of this, probably because the average man is himself so susceptible to the alluring power of gold. One of the traditional taunts hurled at the minister is—"the bigger the salary the louder the call." Now a layman may legitimately exchange one position for another if by so doing he increases his income without the sacrifice of important interests; but this in a minister is by many people counted reprehensible, even positively disgraceful. There is in many quarters a jealous solicitude lest ministers get more money than they ought to have and think more highly of their salary than they ought to think.

But this accusation is not justified. Ministers, as a rule, are not abnormally fond of money. No other set of men in all the world think so little about it, or care so little for it. That a man is in the ministry is presumptive evidence that he does not worship the golden calf. What a dunce a man would be to go into the ministry for the sake of making money! Is not the average minister's salary pitifully small, and are not thousands of salaries a disgrace to the church? Every man who goes into the ministry takes, in reality, the vow of poverty. He turns his back on all the avenues which lead to wealth. He surrenders all hope of ever becoming a rich man. No man in this country has ever become rich in money by his service as a minister. Occasionally a minister comes into possession of wealth, but it is not through his salary as a pastor of a church. There is only the smallest fraction of ministers whose salaries are

large, and these few are large to meet the extrava-
gant expensiveness of living in great cities. When,
therefore, the critics accuse ministers of having
an itching palm, they deal in calumny. That in
this money-loving, money-seeking, money-crazy
world a multitude of young men are every year
turning their backs on the glittering financial in-
ducements held out by other callings and dedi-
cating themselves to a profession which dooms
them to be poor is one of the sublimest phenom-
ena of our century, and an indisputable proof that
the Spirit of God is still among us.

But covetousness does not necessarily mean
love of money. It is an excessive desire for anything which gratifies one's own cravings. It is the
disposition for having and for getting. Money is
not the only thing which can be had or gotten,
and the very fact that money is shut out from the
possible acquisitions of the minister possibly
makes him more covetous for those things which
do lie within his reach. Covetousness is a part of
our unregenerate human nature, and if it cannot
exert itself in one direction it endeavors to make
conquests in another. When one speaks of the
salary of the minister, he should not stop with
the sum of money which the minister annually
receives. Money is only one element in the
minister's annual stipend. He is paid money, and
also gratitude, and praise, and applause, and
admiration. He is given not only dollars, but social privileges and positions which are worth

more to a man of culture than banknotes. He has opportunities for study and self-cultivation, for meditation, and for those quiet pursuits in which the studious nature takes delight. Compensations come to him which are more valuable than rubies; satisfactions subtle and sweet are his which the man of the world knows nothing about. While in one sense the minister is the poorest-paid man in the community, in another sense no man is so generously rewarded. The minister who is really called of God to lead men in the way of life has a remuneration which cannot be computed in the terms of our earthly arithmetic, and which he would not exchange for the income of the highest-salaried man in the town.

It is right here, then, that the pastor meets one of his two most dangerous temptations. He is tempted to make himself the center of the church, and like a medieval baron exact illicit tribute from the people. A Puritan preacher once declared that "a covetous person lives as if the world were made altogether for him, and not he for the world." Are there not ministers who, according to this definition, are covetous? Do they not often think and act as though the church were made for them? Men sometimes come out of the seminary with no conception of Christian servantship, no idea that the church is to be first always, no notion that the church does not exist for the pastor but that the pastor exists for the church.

There is nothing more dismaying than the tone

of the talk in which some ministers indulge. They confess quite blandly that they are looking for a church that will pay them a living salary while they carry out a cherished plan. The church they are looking for must be in a certain locality, must pay a certain salary, must have a certain kind of parsonage, and must be made up of a certain type of people. Sometimes ministers speak of their personal schemes unabashed and without a blush, and go into their first church with no other thought uppermost in their mind but that of their own personal advantage. When such a man gets a church, the tragedy begins. He lays out a line of study according to his own taste. He delves in fields to which his intellectual proclivities carry him. He finishes certain investigations, perhaps, which were begun in school. He gives himself to sundry branches of philosophy or science for which he has a liking. As for the people, who are they? They ought to be satisfied with anything. Every sermon has something in it, and it is the business of laymen to find what that something is. Sunday after Sunday the hungry sheep look up and are not fed.

A church going to pieces through sheer neglect while its appointed leader is dabbling in outside ventures is a spectacle which brings pain to the heart of every true lover of God and must cause anguish among the angels in heaven. Sometimes the church is used simply as a steppingstone to something better. A minister goes into a church with no desire to extend Christ's kingdom there, but solely for the purpose of stepping at the earliest opportunity from that church into one more nearly level with his deserts. Such men are, as a rule, shockingly conceited.

Covetousness is a soil in which all sorts of briers and brambles grow. If the poison of covetousness flows in a man's blood, there is no limit to the foolish things he will think and do. By brooding on himself, he generates an abnormal estimate of his worth. Nothing is too good for him. He thinks the highest pulpit in the land hardly worthy of him. He is always aspiring to churches forever beyond him. He thinks he is going to be called by committees who have never once thought of him, and never will. His dreams are pitiable and also disgusting. This is one of the elements in the awful retribution which God inflicts on those who profess to follow in the steps of Jesus and who are really living solely for themselves.

Throughout the country there are, here and there, sour and disgruntled ministers, their hearts in constant ferment, all because they have been denied that recognition which, in their opinion, their shining merits indisputably deserve. They speak with scorn of "favored brethren" who, without half their intellectual resources, and with only a fraction of their merit, have by means of influential friends or chance, or possibly the devil, succeeded in outstripping them. How reprehensible! "Put to death covetousness," says the Apostle Paul, "it is idolatry." The idolatry of self always leads to spiritual ruin, and never so swiftly as when the sinner is a minister.

Covetousness leads to conceit and also to vanity. Every human being has in his heart a peacock, and the peacock is ever hungering after crumbs. The covetous man feeds the peacock in him all the time. People praise his sermons, and this praise makes him voracious for more praise. They compliment his voice, or his memory, or his beautiful diction, and this wakens an appetite which, growing by what it feeds on, is never satisfied. This abnormal love of praise is in reality a form of covetousness. It is a sort of avarice which is as fatal as the greed for money. Praiseful words are coins, and some men itch and burn for them as other men do for silver and gold. Sometimes this disease makes such progress that the poor man becomes an object of ridicule in the church. He seeks habitually for compliments, and every man whose heart is sound secretly despises him. The last man of all men upon the earth who ought to hunger after the sugar of popular commendation is the minister of Jesus of Nazareth. If the applause-seeking brother were not spiritually asleep, he would hear a voice saying: "How can you believe, who receive honor from men and seek not the honor which comes from God only?"

Covetousness has still another sprout—carelessness. A man who thinks too much about himself has not sufficient time to give thought to others. Self is a big subject and, when one goes into it, there is no getting through with it. The covetous man is sure to become neglectful of those forms of work which are distinctively pastoral. Ministering in the homes of the sick and the poor, work that involves quiet and obscure labor which no one but God sees—it is here that the covetous minister shows what manner of man he is. There are, obviously, many duties which a minister cannot escape. No matter how covetous he may be, he will attend to these, for these make for his advantage. He cannot stay away from a wedding, or absent himself from a funeral, or remain at home from a prayer meeting, or go off on a visit over Sunday. Public duties hold him as in a vise. Even the worst of men will do things which are for their profit.

It is therefore in the doing or not doing of private duties that a minister's true self is disclosed. If he be selfish, he need not go today to call on the woman who is ill; he can go tomorrow. The world will not know. If she dies tonight, she will never tell that he did not come. He need not go out of his way to comfort a man who lost his only son last month. An omission of that sort never gets into the papers. The outsider living without hope and without God in the world has no open claim on him, but the claim of the last magazine is imperious—and therefore he can give time to the magazine to the neglect of the outsider. Looking up a member of his church who has grown negligent is, likewise, not so congenial a task as many another. The wandering sheep does not want to be looked after. Why pester him with pastoral attention? The town will go on just the same with one less sheep in the fold. Similarly, a bad boy who is breaking his mother's heart needs a bit of admonition, but if he does not get it, he will not divulge the pastor's neglect. A hundred little things ought to be attended to, but every little thing eats up energy and time, and even though these little things are really important things in the lives of human beings, they are matters that can be omitted without the minister being called to account. It makes a vast difference in the tone and trend of church life whether the minister is faithful in that which is little, or whether he devotes himself solely to the things which are conspicuous and big.

Yes, a considerable part of pastoral work can be slighted without the lightning falling. Many of the finest and most critical things can be neglected without bringing the minister to open shame; but when a pastor allows things to run at loose ends in his church and is careless in his response to obscure but vital needs, he may win golden opinions from many sorts of people but he rests under the condemnation of the Good Shepherd.

Covetousness also manifests itself often in cowardice. A covetous man, as a rule, runs at the sight of a wolf. A man careful of himself has no fondness for danger. He will save himself, whosoever else may be lost. A crisis arises in the church and he hands in his resignation. Enemies of the flock have appeared, and in the hour when the people most need guidance, the leader abdicates his position. A great moral question is at issue, but he is afraid to come out boldly for the truth and the right. When skies were blue he seemed brave enough, but when the storm burst he was the first to seek cover. In days of peace he blew a furious blast calling the cohorts to battle, but when the enemy appeared he slunk ignominiously from the field. This was because he was a covetous man. He was abnormally fond of his own skin. Covetousness is one of the most subtle and deceitful of all sins.

It would be impossible to paint with colors too black the enormity of the sin of covetousness in the envoys of the Son of God. Nothing is so destructive of the Christian faith as a selfish minister. There are laymen whose faith has been destroyed forever by the unworthiness of their pastor. They once had high confidence in Christian ministers and were foremost workers in the church, and then, alas, one day there came a minister who, preaching with his lips the gospel of unselfishness, had behind his preaching the rank corruption of an avaricious spirit. Little by little it became revealed that the minister was working for himself, that the welfare of the church was not in all his thoughts. And when the crisis came, he sacrificed the church to secure his own advancement.

When laymen have at their head a covetous leader, they oftentimes say nothing—they sicken spiritually and die. They lose their faith in their minister, and then their faith in all ministers. They lose their interest in their church, and finally in all churches. Woe to the minister who by his selfish heart not only loses heaven himself but closes the door so that others cannot enter—he is the worst man in the church; he is worse than a robber. A robber may wrong his victim and still retain a certain sense of honor. Robbery may be his business, and with open face he may acknowledge his unwillingness to be an honest man. But a minister who lives for self is not only a robber but a sneak. He pretends to live for others, and if under his pretense he lives solely for himself, he is the most despicable of all rascals. He is the steward of heavenly treasures, and if he looks out mainly for himself, he is recreant to the highest trust which God commits to men. He is a leading citizen of the heavenly Jerusalem, and if at the expense of others he works for his personal aggrandizement, he is a traitor to the kingdom of God.

Jesus has a name for the covetous preacher. He calls him a hireling. "A hireling," he says, "is not a shepherd at all." He lacks the shepherd's heart and cannot do the shepherd's work. A hireling is a man who works exclusively for pay, his eyes are ever on his wages, his deepest motive is gain. He is always counting up his profits. His god is self. It is amazing how the breath of Jesus has glorified certain words forever. "Servant," for instance, has never been the same since Jesus spoke it, nor has "love." He gave some words a luster which will outlast the stars. Other words, however, he tarnished and left them to make their way down the centuries disgraced and branded. One such word is "hypocrite"; another is "hireling." One cannot speak the word "hireling" free from the accent which Jesus gave it. We cannot make it a sweet and adorning word. We cannot lift it to the seats of the respectable. It is a degraded word, and when we wish to condemn a man, we call him a hireling. He is a man whose heart is not in his work. He does it solely for what he expects to get out of it. Jesus sketches the robber and the hireling side by side in his shepherd allegory. But there is no doubt for which of the two men he had the deeper abhorrence. One can almost catch the scorching hiss of moral detestation in this sentence: "He fleeth because he is a hireling, and careth not for the sheep."

It is noteworthy that Peter in his instructions to shepherds should warn them against the sin of covetousness. "Tend the flock of God, not for filthy lucre, but with a ready mind." The exhortation must have been called for by something which the apostle saw in the lives of church officials. Already that sly serpent, covetousness, had crawled into the garden of the Lord, and was working havoc in the hearts of the Lord's anointed. It is equally striking that Paul in his pastoral address to the elders of Ephesus should say this: "I coveted no man's silver or gold or apparel. Ye well know that these hands ministered unto my necessities, and to them that were with me. In all things I gave you an example, that so laboring ye ought to help the weak, and to remember the words of the Lord Jesus, that he himself said, It is more blessed to give than to receive."

In his first letter to Timothy, Paul lays it down as one of the essential qualifications of a bishop, or shepherd, that he shall be no lover of money. By money, here, we are to understand *every* earthly thing which men count a treasure. There were in apostolic days no comfortable parsonages, no delightful studies, no richly filled bookshelves, no ministerial discounts, no famous pulpits, no eulogizing organizations, no fawning society, no applauding world. Ministers were reviled, persecuted, defamed, made as the filth of the world, the offscouring of all things. There was only one earthly blessing which it was possible for them to covet, and that was money. "Do not set your heart on it," pleaded Peter and Paul. And if they were speaking to ministers today they would say: "Do not set your heart on the earthly advantages which are offered by the ministerial office—time for study, quiet for meditation, opportunity for self-culture, compliments of women, gratitude of men, applause of the world; do not make these the burden of your heart's desire." And the Master would add: "Beware of covetousness. A man's life consists not in the abundance of the things which he possesses."

But the love of things is not more deep-seated or destructive than is the love of power. The love of power is innate in the souls of men. The man is maimed who does not have it. All virile and vigorous men are ambitious. It would be strange if ministers of the gospel had no ambition. The love of prominence, the craving for distinction, the desire for exalted rank, these are deep-seated instincts in our human nature, and a course of study in theology does not eliminate them. Like all the native appetites of the soul they may become abnormal, bringing to their victims suffering and death. No other sin has wrought such havoc among the ministers of Christ as the inordinate love of place and power.

What is the story of a thousand years of Church history but the tragic narrative of how the ministers of Christ, little by little, compacted themselves into a hierarchy which became at last the most blighting and intolerable despotism that the world has ever known? The tyranny of the medieval church was the tyranny of clergymen. Laymen were crowded out of the place appointed them by the Church's founder. Reduced to mere spectators, they had no voice whatever in the government of the church, all authority being gathered up into the hands of ecclesiastics. Rising rank above rank, they formed a compact organization culminating in one supreme head who claimed authority transcending that of the mightiest of the Caesars. His agents, distributed throughout the world, lorded it over the consciences of men, gathering into their clutches all the kingdoms of life. It is the supreme tragedy of Christian history that this ecclesiastical passion for power in the medieval church brought a disgrace upon the cause of Christ from which it will not recover for another thousand years.

The whole world suffers today because of what medieval clergymen did. The cause of Christ is hampered everywhere because of the prejudice planted in the human heart as a result of the imperious and high-handed policy of the ambitious leaders of the Church of Rome. The stories of that tyranny are the property of all mankind. Wherever the name of Jesus is preached, the enemies of Jesus unroll the record of the ambition and cruelty and despotism of the ordained ministers of Jesus, and thereby close the hearts of many.

With the history of the Church open before him, every young man preparing for the ministry has a warning which he should heed as coming straight from heaven. Those clergymen of bygone days were men of like passions as ourselves. They did not start out intending to disgrace and

ruin the Church of God. They were not conscienceless enemies of Christ. They had good reasons for formulating their plausible policies, and
they were able by specious reasoning to justify
all they did. They were not wholly depraved and
reprobate. In their hearts was many a noble aspiration, and in their generation they did many
noble deeds. But alas, ambition, the sin by which
the angels fell, gradually darkened the mind of
the clergy and led it into courses which well-nigh
wrecked the world.

We are Protestants and have broken away from
the despotism of Rome. We rejoice and call ourselves free men in Christ; we believe in the priesthood of believers, in the brotherhood of the
Lord's disciples. We recognize the danger of
church hierarchies; we are on our guard against
every increase of ecclesiastical authority; we
know that the minister of Christ, if dominated
by theories of priestcraft, is the most dangerous
enemy which humanity has to face. And yet
while thus open-eyed to historic facts and teachings, we may be blind to the evil forces working
in our own hearts. Self-assertion, lordly preten-
sion, autocratic temper are not confined to any
one branch of the Christian Church. Protestant-
ism has not escaped entirely the despotism and
the ways of Rome. The old virus still runs in human blood, and today, as always, the old injunc-
tion is timely: "If any man thinks he stands, let
him take heed." We cannot play the monarch in

the splendid and dashing way of the medieval bishop, but it is possible for a Protestant minister to be as insolent as the lordliest of cardinals and as despotic as the most tyrannical of popes. If one were to go up and down our Protestant world, noting carefully the sins of clergymen, would he not write down in his list such as these: autocratic manner, imperious temper, consequential air, dictatorial disposition, self-assertion, hankering after distinction, ambition for higher place, arrogant presumption, refined but earthy lordliness? Every man has in him the elements out of which Rome built a despotism which enslaved the world.

It is worth noting how many things conspire to develop in the minister a proud and imperious disposition. His relation to Christ the Son of God, the consciousness that he is the ambassador of the King of kings, tends to give him a sense of dignity which may easily pass into a vice. The fact that he is entrusted with the oracles of God and is ordained to minister in holy things separates him from men engaged in secular occupations; and this, if dwelt on, has a tendency to beget the feeling, "I am holier than thou."

One wonders, sometimes, how much the shepherd metaphor may be to blame for the exaggerated notions of ministerial prerogative. A metaphor, like every other good thing, is always dangerous. It may be carried too far. The shepherd idea, if rightly used, is illuminating, but if abused it is false and dangerous. It can be construed in such a way as to imply that laymen are weak and silly creatures while clergymen are wonderful beings endowed with supernatural powers, enjoying unique and exclusive favors from heaven. Never did Jesus use the word "sheep" in a depreciatory or disparaging sense. He called little children "lambs" because "lamb" is a love name for a child. He called grown people "sheep" because the word was dear to Hebrew ears, and his countrymen had been singing for centuries: "We are his people, and the sheep of his pasture." Literally speaking, men are not sheep at all. They do not belong to an order of creation lower than that to which the shepherd belongs. The life of pastor and people is on the same level. There is no gulf between the minister and his flock. Pastor and people are members of the same family. They have the same natures and the same privileges. All alike have free access to the throne of grace; all alike are redeemed by the Son of God; all alike are heirs of immortality. It is possible, however, for ministers so to use the shepherd metaphor as to exalt themselves at the expense of the laity and to set up pretensions which are expressly ruled out by the Good Shepherd.

Whatever the influence of the shepherd metaphor may have been, there is no doubt the nature of the preacher's work has a tendency to feed his love of rulership and to quicken his appetite for absolute dominion. What liberty a minister enjoys in the disposition of his time! No other man but the retired millionaire is such a monarch of his day as is the minister. He can read on Monday morning, or write, or walk, or mingle all three, just as he deems best. On Tuesday morning he can attend to his correspondence, or catalogue his library, or eat the heart out of some new book, or meet a company of friends, just as he decides. The order of his going out and coming in is largely at his own discretion. Within wide limits he is the monarch of all the hours he surveys. Such liberty is dangerous; it has spoiled its thousands.

His dominion over his sermons is still more wonderful. He is free to say what the text shall be, the topic, the illustrations, the arguments, the conclusion, and no one can interfere. He can adopt any style of preaching that he likes; he can follow whatever line of thought he chooses. A merchant has to give his customers what they ask for; a hotel-keeper must supply what his guests desire. But a preacher can give what he thinks his hearers ought to want and ought to have, no matter what their needs and wishes really are. For half an hour or more every Sunday morning everything is silent while he speaks. This unparalleled immunity from the noises and interruptions and contradictions which other men are subject to begets in certain types of men a tone of mind which says: "I am Sir Oracle, and when I open my lips, let no dog bark."

In social life a minister is ever at the front. He is the one observed by all observers. Wherever he sits is the head of the table. He has his critics and detractors, but they are not visible at social functions. In social life, especially in small towns, there is a deference paid to ministers which no other man receives. This burning of incense before the minister has a tendency in many cases to turn his head, and to lead him to think more highly of himself than he ought to think. Is there a celebration in the town? The minister must attend it. Is the fitting word to be spoken on a state occasion? The minister must speak it. Here is a true description of ministers not a few: "They love the chief places at feasts and the chief seats in the synagogues, and the salutations in the market-places, and to be called by men, Rabbi." They love these things because they are human and because they are accustomed to them, and because they think they have a right to them. Constant deference and obedience have a tendency to beget in men of a certain grade a haughty and unlovely disposition.

But mightiest of all the forces working for the undoing of the minister's heart is the liberty he has in devising and shaping the policy of the church. Laymen, as a rule, are too busy to take continued interest in church affairs. The result is that in many churches almost everything is rolled upon the pastor's shoulders. It was in this way that church government blossomed into

Romanism. The laity in the early Christian centuries were largely ignorant, incompetent and indifferent, and the whole shaping and managing of the church fell inevitably into the hands of its clerical officials. Laymen in our day are not ignorant or incompetent, but many of them are indifferent because they are so busy. They have no time to bother with church affairs. Church administration is left, therefore, largely in the hands of the pastor. This is bad for him, and it is bad also for the church. It makes it easier for the minister to build up in himself a dictatorial disposition and to nourish in his heart the love of autocratic power.

Note some of the ways in which this lordliness of temper shows itself. It is manifested sometimes in the tone of the sermon. There is too much of the magisterial and not enough of the friendly. There is too much omniscience, and not enough of the humility which Jesus loves. Truth, to go in, need not be driven in. Sledge hammers are not essential for the introduction of ideas. Keats once said, "Poetry should be great, but unobtrusive." So ought a sermon. It ought to be great, but it ought not to obtrude itself. If men go away saying, "That was a great sermon," it falls short of the ideal. When men listened to Demosthenes, they did not go off saying, "That was a great oration." They said: "Let us march against Philip."

There are, moreover, preachers who by the expression of their face, the poise of their body, and the character of their gestures say quite plainly: "This is God's truth! Do not dare to deny it! Take it! Take the whole of it! Take it immediately!! By the Eternal, I will *make* you take it!!!" It is not necessary, however, to put grass into the sheep's mouth. Cram the grass down the sheep's throat, and the animal is so flustered he will not eat at all. Put the grass within reach of the sheep, and he will eat it himself. So it is with truth. Hold it up so that people can plainly see it; bring it within comfortable reach of them; give them time to get at it, and they will eat it. Charles Lamb used to say that "the truth of a poem ought to slide into the mind of the reader while the reader is imagining no such thing." The truth of the sermon ought to glide into the mind of the hearer without the hearer really knowing what is going on.

It is not an encouraging sign when men go away saying, "What a tremendous fellow that is! What a mighty effort that was!" It is better when they think nothing of the preacher, but go away with a heart disquieted by the memory of things they have done amiss and teased by the haunting image of a bright ideal. A heavenly perfume should hang round their spirit as sweet as that which filled the room in which Mary poured the oil upon the Master's head. Dictators are out of place in the pulpit. Dictatorship is a form of carnal striving after power.

This ecclesiastical lordliness shows itself sometimes in the tone of condescension with which

opponents are dealt with, and the haughty inso-
lence with which skeptics are brushed aside. The
supercilious and scornful ease with which unbe-
lieving philosophers and materialistic scientists
are attacked and overwhelmed by young men,
and old men too, in the pulpit is a sad exhibition
of an unchristian spirit. The fact that these opponents of the Christian faith cannot be present to
make reply lays upon the minister an extra responsibility to be scrupulously fair in all his quotations and beautifully just in all his judgments.
To rush furiously upon the ideas of a famous and
learned man who is hundreds of miles away and
hold these ideas up to flippant ridicule when the
man can neither explain nor defend himself is not
the action of a gentleman.

The same derisive spirit sometimes exhibits itself in the vociferous defense of orthodoxy. Every minister is of course under bonds to proclaim
and defend what he conceives to be the truth, but
he is also under bonds to proclaim the truth in
love. No man is doing anything for the advancement of the religion of Jesus whose heart is
vindictive and bitter and who attacks alleged error by misrepresenting men who differ from him.
Every generation brings forth a company of stal-
wart champions who assume that they alone are
the true custodians of the truth. These high and
mighty ones, to whom the slaughtering of the
heretics has been entrusted, are not really prophets, speakers for God; they speak for them-

selves. It was when Elijah had a swollen head over his victory at Carmel that he conceived the idea that he alone in Israel had not bowed the knee to Baal.

In the realm of church administration a puffed-up shepherd exhibits symptoms which have been often deplored. He resents all divergence from his opinions. Men who do not agree with him are set down as his foes. He treats them as traitors to the cause of truth. All who will not carry out his wishes have the mark of the beast. He is irritated by the least opposition. He is mortified by the failure of a single plan. Any independence of thought he considers a personal affront. If a household refuses to receive him, he calls down fire from heaven upon it. Strong in a clear conscience, he proceeds to break down opposition by the force of his ingenuity. He schemes to get ahead of the insurgents by adroit management. He succeeds—but success can be bought at too heavy a price. The price is always too heavy when success is bought at the expense of the highest Christian spirit in the heart of the shepherd.

Many a minister has in the church meeting made a great triumph, only to discover the next day that he was overthrown. A majority of votes were secured for his project, but that amounted to nothing because of the number of hearts which were estranged. A minister may carry his measure and at the same time lose his cause. What cannot be secured by sweet persuasion had better be gone without. It is only a bully who tries to tyrannize or club people into advocating his projects, and the minister who attempts it is a man whose heart has been eaten out by the overweening love of power. It is a good thing for a minister to be defeated now and then, in order to find out that he is not invincible and that there are other people in the world besides himself. Victory is often only by way of the cross. A good shepherd ought not to shrink from an occasional crucifixion.

A little Protestant despot, a petty parochial pope, is a sorry caricature of a minister of Jesus Christ. A minister who boasts under his breath that he proposes to run things and who chuckles at his adeptness in manipulating people, and who says by his manner that he is the boss of the church, is a man who is a stumbling-block in the way of Christian progress. If to the minister the people are only silly sheep, fit for nothing but to be shorn now and then, he is certain to put on airs and bring the Christian ministry into disrepute. He will scold in the prayer meeting, play the part of a dictator on Sunday, move with a patronizing air among the poor and a supercilious smirk among the rich, give orders in a loud voice to all the officials in the town—while wise men blush for his folly and the church mourns the loss of a leader who, because he has not the spirit of Christ, no longer models the Master he ostentatiously professes to serve.

The pastor is possessor of a power that is extraordinary, and hence he must be evermore on his guard against the temptation to play the lord. Peter, in writing to the pastors in his day, said: "Tend the flock of God, not as lording it over the charge allotted to you, but making yourselves examples to the flock." In other words, your power is not denied. No man can take it from you; it is given you by God himself. Be careful how you use it. Do not strut. Do not clothe yourself in pomp. Do not play the tyrant in your sacred robes. Exert your power in the ways that the Lord has appointed. Exercise dominion after the Lord's own fashion. Be a pattern man after which men can shape their lives. Be a model toward which the people can ever look. Be an example through which the power of Christ can reach and transform the hearts of men. This is the charge given by the leader of the twelve, and he got his instructions from the Chief Shepherd.

In the training of the apostles there was no virtue so often extolled and insisted on as humility. The twelve were intensely human, and under the influence of Jesus' personality and ideas new ambitions awakened in them, and they began to dream of lofty places which they were going to fill in the coming kingdom. It is one of the mysteries of sin that men can have their minds filled with thoughts of self-abnegation and unselfishness and at the same time be dreaming of preeminence and power. The men who were with

Jesus at Caesarea Philippi and heard his words about the coming tragedy of the cross began immediately to discuss the old, fascinating and tormenting question, which of them was to be the greatest. They were not sinners above all others; we are men of like nature with them. We too can listen to the words of Jesus about humility and self-renunciation, and repeat them to our people, and at the same time nurse in our hearts ambitions to climb and shine and dominate.

There are certain passages in the Gospels especially appropriate for ministers, paragraphs which ought to be read again and again in the inner chamber when the door is shut. One of them is the eighteenth chapter of Matthew's Gospel, with its story of Jesus summoning the twelve and taking a little child and setting him in their midst, and saying: "Except ye be converted, and become as little children, ye shall not enter into the kingdom of heaven. Whosoever, therefore, shall humble himself as this little child, the same is greatest in the kingdom of heaven." The simplicity and unpretentiousness of an unspoiled child is a revelation of what Christ expects in his ministers.

A second classic passage is Matthew the twenty-third chapter. "Be not ye called Rabbi: for one is your Teacher and all ye are brethren. Call no man your father on the earth: for one is your Father, even he who is in heaven. Neither be ye called masters: for one is your Master, even the

Christ. He that is greatest among you shall be your servant. Whosoever shall humble himself shall be exalted." There is a danger lurking in titles. The word which Rome selected for her priests has had much to do with perpetuating her error and riveting her power. It is not good for ministers to be called by their people "Father." It is not good for the ministers themselves. It assumes a dignity and prerogative in the minister which do not exist, and an immaturity and dependence in the people which are not normal or wholesome. Ministers are not teachers in the sense in which Christ is a Teacher. They are not masters in the way in which Christ is a Master. They are his representatives, but they do not take his place nor possess his power. There is but one Lord, Jesus Christ, God's Son.

A third chapter for pastors is the thirteenth chapter of the Gospel of St. John. The tragedy in the upper chamber is one of the darkest in human history. The twelve men who have spent years in the close companionship of the most unselfish man who ever lived, enjoying the illumination of his teaching and the cleansing power of his prayers, are still so petty and so selfish at the very end of their Master's life that they cannot sit down to partake of a farewell dinner without childish squabbling over the order of their places at the table. It was when their hearts were feverish and resentful that Jesus took the basin and the towel and proceeded to wash the disciples' feet. After the work was completed, he said: "Ye call me Teacher and Lord; and ye say well, for so I am. I have given you an example that you also should do as I have done to you. If ye know these things, blessed are ye if ye do them." From the upper room Jesus went to the garden of Gethsemane, and from Gethsemane to the cross. It made men laugh to see a king crucified. They had never seen a king without a plume and without a crown. He was crucified, but King he was, and is, and shall be forever. From his cross he rules the world.

In his hands he holds all souls. His claim upon no one of them has ever been relinquished. He is the Shepherd, and all the sheep are his. The minister speaks of his church, his people, his parish— and this is proper if he understands the meaning of his words. As distinguished from one another, one parish belongs to one man and another parish belongs to another man, but in the deep sense all parishes alike belong to Christ The human shepherds come and go in a continuous procession. A minister arrives in town, unpacks his books, does his work, and then sleeps with his fathers. "He cometh up and is cut down like a flower; he fleeth as it were a shadow, and never continueth in one stay." But Jesus Christ is the same yesterday, today, and forever. He is with his people even unto the end of the world.

When Jesus handed over to Simon Peter the charge of the Christian Church, he was careful to use the possessive pronoun "my." "Feed my lambs! Tend my sheep! Feed my sheep!" It is the mightiest pronoun in the New Testament for the saving of the minister from lordliness. "Simon, son of Jonas, feed my lambs. They are not yours, they are mine, but I wish you to look after them for a little while. Tend my sheep. They are not yours. I do not give them to you. They belong to me. Mine they always shall remain, but I ask you to tend them for a season for me. Feed my sheep. They are not yours. Not one of them shall ever pass from my possession, but I am going away for a few days and I leave them with you. Guard them, feed them, guide them, be good to them for my sake. Follow me. Remember my gentleness, my watchfulness, my considerateness, my patience, my compassion, my readiness to help, my swiftness to heal, my gladness to sacrifice. Be the kind of shepherd to my lambs and my sheep that I have been to you. Follow me!"

Chapter 5

The Shepherd's Reward

A certain school of ethics would question the wisdom of adding this subject to our list. "Virtue is its own reward," we are told, "and to inquire what one is going to get for doing his duty is vitiating. Work is better and the heart is nobler when one gives no thought to the recompense of his toil. We ought to do what we do with an eye single to the doing of it, with no demand for or anticipation of pay." It is a lofty-sounding philosophy, but it is too high-flown for healthy-minded mortals. It is a fetish that comes from the pit. The New Testament knows nothing of the danger of looking to the end. Jesus never shrank from talking about results. For the joy that was set before him he endured the cross, despising the shame. In the presence of his disciples he prayed, "I glorified thee on the earth, and now, Father, glorify thou me." The prophet declared that the Messiah would see the travail of his soul and be satisfied.

In all his teachings Jesus leaves no unfinished pictures. If he paints a sower sowing seed, he paints also the harvest growing golden in the sun. If he pictures wheat and tares, he also pictures the barn and the fire. If he sketches men working in a vineyard, he sketches them at evening time receiving, each man, his wages. When he portrays Dives at the banquet, he is careful to tell what Dives deserves and gets. He does not fail to inform us what is the ultimate fate of the men entrusted with the talents. He gives men reasons for doing well, and assures them that they are going to receive praise or condemnation according to their deeds. When Peter asked Jesus what he was going to receive by way of recompense for the sacrifices he had made, Jesus did not rebuke him, but assured him that "there is no man that hath left house, or brethren, or sisters, or mother, or father, or children, or lands, for my sake, and for the gospel's sake, but he shall receive a hundredfold now in this time, houses, and brethren, and sisters, and mothers, and children, and lands, with persecutions; and in the world to come eternal life." What does this mean but that the ministers of Christ are to be richly rewarded for their labors. They are to receive the very best things in this world and still better things in the next. What is promised is in every generation beautifully fulfilled.

A minister who does his work with an eye single to God's glory, leaving everything else behind, receives the best things the world affords. A multitude of people become his relatives and friends. Fathers and mothers are as proud of him as though he were a member of their family. Old men look down on him lovingly as on a son. Young men look up to him reverently as to a father. Men of his own age love him as a brother. A large circle feel that in him they have a comrade and a friend. He enjoys free access to many homes. Houses and lands are his, not by legal title, but by spiritual prescription. Appreciation, gratitude, affection—these are the gold, frankincense, and myrrh constantly poured out before him. If love is the best thing in the world, then the faithful pastor gets more of the earth's richest treasure than any other man. This is his first reward.

To be sure, he will not be loved by everybody. Jesus was careful to state that the good things would be accompanied by tribulations. These also are a part of the minister's reward. The Pharisees and Sadducees and scribes will always be against him. Men not bad at heart but of stupid ear will misunderstand him and misrepresent him. The idler will gossip about him and the ungrateful will return evil for good. Those possessed of demons will openly attack him. All this is to be expected. Is the pupil to be above his teacher, and the servant above his master? Think it not strange, young men, when this fiery experience overtakes you. Do not be thrown into panic because all men do not speak well of you. Do not cry and sob when you meet with opposition in your church. Do your duty and you will stir up trouble, but you will never be left without faithful hearts to love you. When you go into Gethsemane, friends will remain praying at the gate, and if you die on the cross you will carry into heaven with you the affectionate devotion of many loyal hearts. There is nothing more beautiful on this earth than the love of a church for a faithful pastor.

There are ministers now alive who feel that it would be worthwhile to toil a thousand years to win such love as they have received. The taunts of Pharisees and the gibes of the chief rulers and the priests are all forgotten by the man who has the affection of a multitude of friends. The petty criticism, to which every man in public place is of necessity subjected, counts for nothing in the long sweep of the years. All the hateful and stinging things which are said by spiteful critics are only a few bubbles borne on the bosom of a tide of love. When a pastor comes near the end of his career, he forgets all about the little gusts of bitterness which have now and then blown across his path, and says with the Psalmist: "Goodness and mercy have followed me all the days of my life."

This love of the pastor is not only beautiful but lasting. It survives when many other things have perished. The affection for a pastor is different from the admiration for a preacher. The preacher, if eloquent, gets brass bands and torchlight processions. He is given newspaper space and applauding crowds, but his fame is speedily forgotten. When his vocal chords fail the crowds disappear, and only here and there is a heart which feels the sense of bereavement. Not so with the pastor. He lives in the hearts of those he has befriended. There is no memory so long-lived as the memory of kindness. Great pulpit efforts are speedily forgotten, famous books soon drop out of the public mind. Who cares to read a book of sermons or of theology published fifty years ago? Authors and orators live in book fame, whereas shepherds live in the hearts of those who were shepherded by them. A man's reputation for eloquence may live long in a community, but his reputation for goodness will live longer.

When one listens to aged people talking about the ministers of their youth, he hears remarks such as these: "I shall never forget how comfortingly he spoke at my mother's funeral." "I often think how he put heart into me at a time when I did not care to live any longer." "I can feel now the touch of his hand on my head when I was yet a mere lad." "I love to remember how kind he was to the poor, and how self-sacrificing he was in the time of the great epidemic." These are the memories which live. The sons of thunder have tongues which fill the world for a fleeting season with silver music, but the James whom the early church remembered was the James who was the first to lay down his life for the Master; and the John who lived longest in Asia Minor was not the theologian or the orator, but the shepherd who wandered off in search of a convert who had become a brigand, refusing to cease his importunate appeals until he had brought the wandering sheep back to the fold. When Phillips Brooks died, the world lost a prince of preachers, but in the weeks immediately succeeding his death it was not stories of his eloquence which were repeated most frequently up and down the Boston streets but stories of his pastoral faithfulness and instances of his kindness in the homes of the poor.

What is in the lives of our parents that we remember best? It is not the theories they advocated, the wise speeches they delivered, the learned papers they read, but rather their unwearied patience, their faithful kindness, and their self-effacing affection for us. These are the memories which linger in our hearts, and when we meditate upon them the heavens open and the angels of God come down.

It is a commendable ambition to wish to live in the hearts of our fellows. The surest way of fulfilling that ambition is to do faithfully a shepherd's work. Many of us cannot be brilliant—we could have been had God so ordered—but we can every one be faithful. We can all be full of helpfulness, we can all have it said of us as it was said of Barnabas, "He was a good man

and full of the Holy Ghost." We can all deserve
to have chiseled on our tomb the simple inscrip-
tion which is to be seen on a solitary grave at the
foot of the Apennines: "He was a good man and
a good guide."

In addition to the love of human beings, the
pastor receives other satisfactions even higher
and more blessed. His second reward is the gratification of helping people, and the peace of mind
which comes at the end of work by which a heart
has been soothed and brightened—the pleasure
of taking men by the hand and lifting them out
of the sloughs of despond, and sometimes out of
the pit of despair. To him the joy is given of
changing the tone and temper of a home. He may
enjoy the rapture of knowing that in the hands
of God he has been instrumental in transforming the life of a community. These are rewards of
a subtle and ethereal sort, coins paid out over the
counters of heaven. They are indescribable and
unspeakable forms of remuneration. The world
cannot give them, nor can the world take them
away. The satisfaction of holding a great congregation attentive for an hour is not to be despised,
but the satisfaction of knowing that by an act of
yours one human life has been changed forever
is a satisfaction infinitely more precious. The
gratification which comes at the end of a public
work successfully achieved is sweet, but infinitely
sweeter is the sense of having been able by the
grace of Christ to turn one man's face toward

God.

The power of personal influence, the ability to pour one's life into another life, is one of the richest of all the gifts of heaven, and this is peculiarly the gift granted to the shepherd. By coming close to the individual soul, the shepherd communicates to that soul something of the essence of his own spirit, and from that time forward he lives not only in himself but also in another soul which by him has been transfigured. He is permitted by the goodness of God to kindle a fire on an altar that was cold and to recreate the world for a heart that had lost the joy of living. Through his patience and wisdom and fidelity, men who have lived without hope and without God in the world are quickened into new life, and begin to glorify their Father who is in heaven. This reward is richer than any other. It is a great thing to win love for oneself, but it is a greater thing to win love for God.

The shepherd can do both. Men will love him as they love no other man in all the world because he has taught them how to love God. Things which eye saw not and which ear heard not and which entered not into the heart of man, but which were prepared for those who work for God, are revealed by the Eternal Spirit to the shepherd heart. The peace that passes understanding is a rich part of a shepherd's pay.

But while the pastor may receive these rich interior rewards, does he not buy them at the price of pulpit efficiency? While he is winning the affection of sundry persons whom he has individually befriended, is he not likely to lose his grip on the crowd? Many a young minister goes into his first church feeling that every hour devoted to pastoral work is lost time. He does such work grudgingly, assuming that it is done at the expense of pulpit power. The assumption is mistaken. No man can study all the time. A few hours a day with books will exhaust the most vigorous brain. One can get more out of books in a half day than in a whole day provided he uses the other half day in a way to sharpen his appetite for fresh reading. Moreover, in pastoral service a minister *is* at work on his sermon! Sermon preparation requires two stages—work on the preacher and work on the message. The first is as important as the second. If the preacher is not prepared, the message will be thin. The more thoroughly cultivated the heart of the preacher, the finer will be the texture and flavor of the sermon. There is no preparation of the preacher comparable with that which he gets in mingling with people. A minister is as truly fitting himself to preach when engaged in pastoral labors as when in his study he has the dictionaries and encyclopedias and commentaries spread out before him.

But is not close contact with the people disillusioning, and thereby injurious to the preacher's enthusiasm? Does not distance lend enchantment to the view, and is not a more intimate knowledge of the pettinesses and meannesses of men apt to chill a speaker's zeal and introduce a pessimistic note into his message? In this case, is not a little knowledge a desirable thing and a more extensive knowledge somewhat dangerous? These assumptions are all incorrect. It is when we touch men with our fingertips that we dislike them. It is when we know them only a little that we are harshest in our judgments. When we come to know them better we discover many good things which we had missed at first. When we understand all which they have suffered, we make allowances for their shortcomings and our heart goes out in sympathy instead of condemnation. Why, moreover, should a minister be estranged by the moral infirmities of men? Why should he be galled by their petty ignorance, or disgusted by their foibles, or enraged by their prejudices, or soured by their vices? If humanity were morally sound, then were there no need of a physician. If men were what they ought to be, there would be no place for pastors. It is because men *are* in a state of ruin that Christ has sent his messengers throughout the world. If a minister finds himself growing cynical, let him drop his pen and associate still more closely with the people. The cure for pessimistic estimates of human nature is not aloofness but closer contact! The most enthusiastic believer in human nature the world has ever had was the man who got the closest to publicans and sinners, and who knew to the uttermost what is in man.

But can one be a thinker and a worker, a man of thought and a man of action? Can a minister be practical and retain the divine impulse? Can he interest himself in mundane details and at the same time soar aloft into the heavens? Does not attention to parochial affairs cripple the wings of the imagination and paralyze the higher powers of the soul? Can a man talk lovingly of heaven with both his feet planted on the earth? The answer is, of course he can. Antaeus stood no chance at all with Hercules save when his feet touched the earth, and no preacher can grapple effectively with the herculean forces of this world unless he stands flatfooted on the plane on which mortals live. The greatest of all poets, Shakespeare, had a practical, matter-of-fact mind. He could interest himself in prosaic matters in little Stratford as well as poetic matters on the London stage. His mind was wide enough to take in the tragic experiences of the heroes and heroines of human history as well as the common work and play of obscure men in English village life. It was because he looked so sympathetically on the plain humdrum life about him that he was able to create characters which will be the joy of the world forever.

Someone may ask whether it is wise for a minister who wishes to become an author to give much time to ordinary pastoral duties. Why not? Doing pastoral work does not fit every man to be an author, for God in his mercy has not ordained that every minister shall write a book. But if a minister is sent into this world to write a book, his pastoral work will only increase his talent. No man has a right to publish a book unless he has learned something which it is worthwhile for the world to know. How can he possess fresh and vitalizing knowledge unless he gets on the inside of men? Books that are made out of books are ordinarily stupid and worthless things. The best books are born in the brains of men who have established an original contact with the world.

Christian history makes it clear that pastoral labor does not destroy the instinct or capacity for writing. The most voluminous of all the Puritan writers was Richard Baxter, and he was the very prince of all the seventeenth century pastors. His best books were written in the years when his pastoral work was heaviest. Few books written in the nineteenth century exerted a wider influence than John Keble's *Christian Year*, and that was written by a village pastor immersed in pastoral cares. George Herbert composed the best of his poems when he was calling on the sick and poor. Charles Kingsley wrote some of his greatest volumes when his pastoral work was so taxing that it was necessary to rise at four or five in the morning in order to find opportunity to use his pen. And John Watson, who charmed the Old World and the New by the humor and pathos of his writings, was one of the most industrious of all the nineteenth century pastors.

In reality, the young minister who, nursing literary ambitions, neglects his pastoral work and shuts himself in his library "all dedicated to closeness and the bettering of his mind," is not likely ever to write a book which the world will care to read. But if a minister seeks first the kingdom of God and does his full duty to his people day by day, then whatever books the Lord has need of will be added to that man. Pastoral work never dulls the pen which God desires to make use of. It was the hard working pastor who carried on his heart the care of all the churches, and who warned every member of the church in Ephesus, night and day, with tears, who was permitted to write a quarter of the New Testament.

But suppose one has an unsocial nature and finds pastoral work a burden; is it legitimate that he coddle himself and let the lambs and sheep suffer? No. If the minister is lacking in social gifts, let him cultivate the social side of his nature more assiduously. If a man has one shoulder higher than the other, the thing to do is not to grow more lopsided but by systematic exercises to bring the lower shoulder up. If a man is timid and awkward in conversation, let him converse more frequently. If he likes subjects better than men, as Nathaniel Burton confessed that he did, let him cultivate men more and more. No effective preacher can be a hermit. When a preacher lives an isolated life, the note of solitariness resounds in his sermons. An unsocial minister needs to be reborn. Why preach the new birth when you do not believe it a possible experience for yourself? Why extol the privilege of becoming a new man in Christ if you persist in remaining the old man, making it impossible for God to work in you any mighty works because of your unbelief?

But can any man be a good preacher and a good pastor at the same time? Does not one gift kill the other? Does not the development of one capacity cause the atrophy of the other? There are ministers who look with jealous eye on their pastoral instincts, fearing that these, if allowed to grow, will paralyze the tongue for preaching. A minister sometimes shrinks from being called a "good pastor," fearing that the compliment disparages him as a preacher and compromises him in the eyes of the public. Such men are deluded. Unless the church is too large, a minister can be good both as pastor and preacher. The better he is as a pastor, the more effective he will be, other things being equal, as a preacher. It is because men limp and crawl in pastoral work that they often stumble and fall in the pulpit. Because they desert the people through the week, God deserts them on Sunday. A man cannot be an ideal preacher unless he has a shepherd's heart.

Here then is a third reward which comes to shepherds: an increase of pulpit power. It is not claimed that every man who proves himself a faithful shepherd will become a famous pulpit orator. Pulpit orators are few—possibly because they are not essential to the progress of the church, and too many of them would corrupt the world. All that is here said is that pastoral work does not snuff out the preaching instinct, and that every man is all the better preacher because of the pastoral work he does, provided that this work is kept within proper limits.

It may be profitable to note a few of the many services which pastoral work renders to the preacher. Perhaps some of you have high ambitions to conquer communities as sons of thunder; it will help you to escape the sin of doing pastoral work with a surly heart if you remember what important and constant contributions pastoral work is making to your sermons. You ought never to do pastoral work grudgingly or of necessity, for God loves a cheerful pastor, and so do the people. Baxter called pastoral work "a sweet and acceptable employment." The labors of a shepherd were to him "not burdens, but mercies and delights." No wonder God's work prospered in his hands.

Let us now consider some of the things which pastoral work does for the preacher.

I. It supplies the minister with material for his sermons. A man who speaks every week to the same people year after year needs an enormous amount of material. It can be gotten out of the parish. The manna falls every day, and it falls near the minister's door. Fresh evidences of the malignity of sin are always being presented. Additional proofs of the presence and guidance of God are every day forthcoming. The best apology for the Christian religion cannot be gotten out of books, but must be framed out of material supplied by the people. The Sea of Galilee is in every church, and Jesus walks along its shore and talks with men and helps them as in the days of old. The minister ought to be there and listen to what the Lord is saying in the experiences of the people. It is there that one enters into the deep things of life.

There are two kinds of profundities: book profundities and everyday profundities. What is matter? What is the relation of matter to spirit? What is the origin of evil? How can the human will be free? What is a tenable definition of inspiration? These are the profundities of books; but the profundities of everyday life are deeper. Love and hate, hope and fear, faith and doubt, sin and duty, forgiveness and remorse, depression and aspiration—into all these the man who would preach with moving power must enter.

It is amazing how many interesting things are being said every day in every parish, and the preacher ought to hear as many of them as possible: original things said by little children, and wise sayings of aged men and saintly women. Hazlitt says, "You will hear more good things in one day on the top of a coach going to and coming from Oxford than in one year from all the residents of that learned seminary." That, of course, is exaggeration, but there is no doubt that good things are to be heard on top of a coach. It is in his parish that the preacher gets his most telling illustrations. It is proper at times to import illustrations just as we import pictures, diamonds, and many kinds of food, but the best illustrations of the preacher are those which are found at his door. Jesus of Nazareth never went out of little Palestine for symbols. It was the seed in the farmer's hands, the wild flower blooming at his feet, the old net lying on the shore, the experiences of men engaged in ordinary occupations, which furnished him pictures by means of which he rendered vivid the realities of the spiritual world.

There come times to every minister when he feels that his material has run out. He has said all he cares to say, he has preached all he knows. The crock has been skimmed so often that no more cream will rise. The tree has been so often shaken that no more fruit will fall. Whenever these barren times arrive, let the minister lock up his study and go forth as a shepherd. Let him walk among his people, observing what is going on. Let him talk to the people who are bearing the burden in the heat of the day. He will find, perhaps, a businessman driven almost to despair by some sudden reversal in fortune, or some woman who is grieving herself into atheism over the death of a child, or some young man who is just entering upon a path that leads down to death, or some young woman who is all perplexed in her first efforts to live a Christian life—and when he gets home he will be in possession of a message. When a preacher finds himself with nothing to say it is because his heart is empty, and the thing to do is to go to the ocean of human need and fill it up again. A preacher always has something to say if he really knows his people.

II. It is in pastoral work that the minister comes to know human nature. His church is the human soul edited up to date. It is not enough to know what the world needs, one must know what it wants. Wants and needs are not the same, and the preacher must know both. It is not sufficient to know the good things which are being said; one ought to know some of the foolish things also, the vices as well as the virtues, the errors as well as the truths. The weaknesses as well as the strong points of the people ought to be clearly apprehended. It is only when the preacher is possessed of this knowledge that he can preach with greatest effect.

No rifleman is likely to hit the target if he fires in the dark. How can a preacher aim a sermon if he does not know where the people are? It is as important that a minister should know his congregation as it is that he should know his Bible. How can he know his congregation unless he meets the people one by one? Walter Scott made

it a practice always to talk with every man with
whom he was casually thrown. He loved to talk
to his servants and the servants of his friends—
gardeners, coachmen, footmen, all sorts of men
were interesting to him. A servant of his once
declared that "Sir Walter speaks to every man as
if he was his blood relation." No wonder Scott
became a wizard who charmed the hearts of millions. By coming close to the human heart, he understood its beat; and when the Waverley novels
appeared, men high and low felt in them the beating of a heart like their own.

The minister who would be an effective
preacher must speak to every man as if that man
were his blood relation. Truth is to be applied—
how can it be applied to men in the dark? Knowledge is to be used—how can it be used wisely
unless one knows the people who are in need of
it? Everything depends on the point of contact,
and this is established in pastoral work.

Matthew Arnold used to call Shelley "a beautiful and ineffectual angel beating in the void his
luminous wings in vain." That is a correct description of many an aspiring preacher. He has
beautiful sentiments, but his message is ineffectual. He speaks with the tongue of an angel, but
he beats in the church atmosphere his sermonic
wings in vain. The cause of the tragedy is his lack
of contact with the world. He is not a shepherd
acquainted with the ways of sheep.

III. Even the form of the sermon can be constantly improved by fidelity in pastoral service. Much in preaching depends on the preacher's vocabulary. It must be made up of words which the people know. The words of the shop and the street and the home are the earthen vessels into which the heavenly treasure is to be poured. Men never understand the gospel unless it is preached to them in the language in which they were born. The temptation of the minister, if he be a lover of books, is to use the words of the scholars rather than the words of the people. Unless he watches himself, he will use words from the Greek or the Latin or the German or the French, when a plain, simple word would do his work better.

Every opaque word subtracts from the preacher's power. A preacher's vocabulary ought to be subjected to the refining influence of ordinary conversation. It is in the suds of everyday speech that the starch of the schools must be washed out of the preacher's style. Style has a tendency to stiffen, and sentences, unless watched, have a fashion of becoming elaborate and complex. If the preacher has fine literary taste he will be tempted to indulge in minute touches, in dainty allusions, in exquisite and intricate phrasings, and in all those delicate gradations of light and shade which are the delight of the exceptional and fastidious and highly cultivated mind. Before he knows it, his style will be a barrier between the people and his truth. The sheep will look toward those wonderful and beautiful sentences, but they will not be fed.

Every preacher needs the disciplinary castiga-
tion of conversation with common people. In conversation one is obliged to be sensible. He cannot put on a silly and artificial tone. If he did,
others would laugh at him and he would probably laugh at himself. If certain preachers could
hear their pulpit tones, they would be exceed-
ingly amused. When we converse, our words are
simple and short, our sentences are straight and
direct, our style is flexible—and hence conversation with plain people is one of the best schools
for the cultivation of an effective pulpit style. The
bane of the pulpit is complex sentences, artificial
arrangement of clauses, and a style that is so
elaborate that the attention lags in trying to ex-
tract the thought from it. All these are burned up
in the fire of conversation. A sermon is defective
if it sounds bookish. It is best when it is nearest
friendly and unstudied talk. Daily intercourse
with all sorts of people will do more to keep a
minister off his pulpit stilts than anything else.

Samuel Johnson at the age of thirty-five wrote
the life of his friend Savage in a style which by
universal consent is abominable. Up to that time
Johnson had lived entirely with books, and his
style was atrociously ponderous and artificial.
When he was seventy, he wrote the *Lives of the
Poets* in a style immeasurably superior to that of
thirty-five years before, and the improvement
was due largely to the fact that as Johnson grew

older he gave himself more and more to conversation with his friends. In conversation much of his early pomp and monotony was sloughed off.

The aim of the preacher is to move men, and he cannot move them with a style like a pair of tongs, long and stiff and hard. Style, to be effective, must be flexible and limp, clear and direct. In a word, it must be conversational. One does not want in the pulpit sitting-room familiarity, but he wants colloquial simplicity and ease. He wants also directness. Sentences must come straight to the individual heart.

Wordsworth says that Dryden composed his poetry without his eye on the object. Wordsworth always kept his eye on the object. That is one reason why Dryden is unread and Wordsworth is popular. Preachers often preach with their eye off the people. This is evident from their language. No man with his eye on the people could possibly go on using a style which is found in many pulpits. Walter Bahehot gives ministers a dig when he says of Coleridge: "Like a Christian divine, he did not regard persons. He went right on, not knowing what was going on in other people's minds." This is a defect which may be remedied by conversing in the homes of the people. Personal intercourse gives directness to thought and clearness to speech. In conversation, style always particularizes and language fits down snug around the individual mind. The preacher who is willing to let his people talk to him through the week will know better how to talk to them on Sunday.

IV. There are still more important things to be gotten from the people—originality, vividness, fire, and the ring of reality. A preacher is nothing if he is not interesting. An uninteresting sermon is a bore. It is not enough, as some imagine, that a sermon be true; it must be true and also interesting. What matters whether it be true or not if people will not listen to it? And they certainly will not listen to it unless it is interesting. A minister who cannot preach interesting sermons was never intended for the pulpit. The first duty of the preacher is to get the attention, and if he cannot get it he might as well go home.

Now, to be interesting a sermon must be original, vivid, and sincere. How can a preacher be original, dealing as he must with themes worn threadbare with the handling of two thousand years? All the doctrines of the Christian faith are commonplace, and every Christian precept is familiar to everybody.* Then how can a sermon be original? Originality lies in the accent with which the sermon is spoken, in the fire in which the sermonic elements have been fused, in the application of the truth which the preacher makes to the people in that particular church. A man, to preach with originality, must have first-hand knowledge of the things of which he speaks. He must look upon the world with his own eyes. He must know

---

* Oh that this were true today! But in any case, originality is still commendable. *Editor*

men at first hand. He must grapple with sin in his own heart and in the hearts of his people. He must know the joys and sorrows, the temptations and triumphs, of the Christian life.

Every man is original who drinks at the fountains of the world's life and does not rely on the cisterns which we call books. The man who mingles with men, and plays with children, and who knows what is going on in his church, will have a vitality and freshness in his speech which will compel people to listen. His thoughts will have a peculiar edge; his message will be vivid. One cannot make a sermon vivid by picking out of the dictionary lurid and picturesque words. A vivid sermon comes out of a feeling heart. A heart that has heat can make dull words incandescent. How can a minister scorch cruelty and injustice unless he has seen them face to face in his own church? How can he abhor the liquor traffic until he has worked with men whom the saloon has finally dragged down to hell? It is first-hand experience with sin which enables men to preach about it, and it is first-hand experience with Christ which makes it possible to tell the old, old story in phrases that etch themselves in fire upon the heart.

Men who hold aloof from the everyday life and suffering of the world may pretend emotion and mimic passion, but their sermons lack the note of reality, and the congregation sits unmoved. A man, to be a preacher, must have an experienc-

ing nature. He must live over in himself the joys
and sorrows through which his people pass. He
must think with them, feel with them, suffer with
them, rejoice with them—only so can the gospel
come from his lips with power. "I preached what
I felt," said John Bunyan. His experience was the
substance of his sermons. This gave them their
life and power. No man really preaches anything
but his experience, that which has become incar-
nate in him, and hence it is impossible for any
man to be a preacher of the first order unless he
bears men's sicknesses and allows the tragedy of
their lives to be relived in his own heart. A shepherd must know his sheep, and then his sheep
will know him.

V. Pastoral work delivers a minister from many
errors and delusions. Robertson used to say, "It
is visitation of the poor which more than anything else brings a man into contact with the actual and the real, and destroys fanciful dreams."
The life of a minister exposes him to many dis-
torting influences, and he needs close contact
with the world of working men and women to
keep him sane and sweet. Two kinds of reading
are today peculiarly misleading: the newspaper
and the theological magazine. The former is gotten up in haste and contains a mass of material
thrown together by young men whose salary depends on their ability to make an interesting
story. The average paper gives a picture of the
world which is lurid, exaggerated, out of propor-

tion, and in false perspective. The world is not half so bad or hopeless as the average paper would make it seem, and the minister needs to correct the newspaper picture by intimate contact with his parish. Some ministers are scandalously pessimistic in their preaching. In the paper one sees chiefly the bad, but in the parish one sees the good as well as the bad—so much of the good that one can thank God and take courage.

The theological magazines and books of biblical criticism deal with a group of problems of great interest to limited circles. The minister who gives too much time to these problems is likely to put an exaggerated emphasis on their importance. The latest theory of a daring German professor, the last speculation of a Dutch or French savant, loom large in the vision of the minister, and he burns, if a conservative, with holy zeal to demolish these new enemies of the faith; or, if he be a radical, to communicate this newfound truth to the people. When the minister comes from the last theological magazine all aglow with enthusiasm over some new interpretation, or with indignation over some wild speculation, let him take a walk among his people and note how indifferent men are to these theological storms. The foolish things in the magazines will never reach his people unless he tells them. The predicted collapse of time-honored doctrines will never pain them if he keeps still. Plausible theories now dominant, but which will be antiquated ten years from now, will not disturb the souls of the faithful if he does not hurl thunderbolts at them from the pulpit.

When one sees a minister demolishing a foreign critic of whom his people have never heard, and demonstrating the falsity of a theory of which his people have never dreamed, and laboriously striving to clear away, in a course of six sermons, stumbling-blocks over which his people have never stumbled, he has an illustration of how foolish a good man can be who reads the magazines more than he reads the lives of his people. Magazines and books have their place, but some ministers are spoiled by them. They give more attention to a few bookworms abroad than they give to the people whom God has entrusted to their keeping.

A minister needs to cultivate his people in order to extend the reach of his Sunday message. The preacher's work is one of persuasion. He cannot force or drive, he can only entice and woo. Success depends not only on the winsomeness of his message but also on the attitude of his hearers. If his hearers are cold or suspicious or critical, he is not likely to persuade them, no matter what he says. If they are kindly disposed toward him, the door of their heart is open and his truth can easily get in. A preacher loses no time when he mingles with men in such a way as to give them confidence in him and to lead them to feel that he has a manly and brotherly heart. Building up in men a responsive disposition, creating in them a friendly and hospitable attitude, this is work which the minister as shepherd does, getting them ready for the message of the minister as prophet. The work of the prophet is to transmit, to convey a message to others.

In the transfer of a truth from one man to another, two things are of supreme importance. The first is that the preacher has a grip on it himself, and the second is that the hearer get a grip on it too. To be sure that the hearer gets a grip on the truth, it is necessary for the preacher to know the hearer's exact position. Treasures cannot be safely handed to men in the dark. The truth which the minister conveys is not to stop with the man who receives it, it is to be handed on. The preacher never reaches his highest success unless his people repeat his sermons. When they repreach his message, his power is increased a hundredfold. Now people will repeat the sermon only of a man they like. They are not apt to love a man who does not love them, and if by his aloofness the minister shows that he does not care for the people, they will not be zealous in passing his sermons on. Lovers delight in repeating the words of the one they love.

It was a beautiful feature of Jewish worship that the high priest should wear upon his breastplate four rows of precious stones, three stones in each row, each stone representing one of the tribes of Israel. In this way all the people were

kept before the high priest in his public minis-
trations. The ideal preacher never goes into the
pulpit without carrying all the people on his
heart. A Russian saint has written suggestively
of the practice of the presence of God. A second
volume might be written on the practice of the
presence of the people. For the preacher, the one
is no less important than the other. If he does not
love to speak to his brethren whom he has seen,
he is not fitted to speak of whom he has not seen.

The fourth and highest reward of the shepherd
is an increase in spiritual stature. Character is the
greatest of all treasures, and character is built by
action. It is the things which one does which de-
termine what he is. "Character forms itself in the
stream of the world." A minister's character is
formed in the stream of church life. It is the things
which he does rather than the books which he
reads which mold his personality and fashion his
disposition. It is his work as a shepherd rather
than his message as a prophet which has most to
do with the enriching of his heart and the refining of his spirit. The reward of the shepherd is
that he becomes increasingly like the Good Shepherd—he is transformed into the same image
from glory to glory even as from the Lord the
Spirit. The minister who watches and guards and
guides men, heals and rescues and feeds them,
develops by his work the virtues and graces of
the Savior himself. What saint is more beautiful
in his old age than the man who for forty or fifty

years has done faithfully the work of the shepherd? One star differs from another in glory, and so do the types of sainthood differ from one another. But for tenderness of heart, and beauty of soul, and Christlikeness of spirit, what character known among men surpasses that of the shepherd saint?

The shepherd-life cultivates a sensitiveness in all the nerves of feeling. The sympathies grow broad, the heart expands and takes in classes which were at first shut out. There is something in preaching which tends to make a man intolerant; one can be so loyal to what he thinks to be the truth as to become hard of heart toward those who will not receive it. Again and again in Christian history the sad spectacle has been presented of a man really entrusted with a message from heaven, but whose fiery devotion to truth closed his heart against those who did not agree with him. The work of the shepherd ever tends to mellow and widen the heart. Working with the lambs, caring for the sick, rescuing the lost, feeding the hungry, all this adds new breadth to the sympathy and helps one to enter more completely into the lives of others. A shepherd whose life has been faithful is sure to be genial in his judgments and indulgent in the allowances which he makes for all classes of men.

The shepherd grows in patience. As long as he lives, his work makes heavy demands on his powers of endurance, but they respond to the call.

The work of a shepherd is full of interruptions, vexations, and disappointments, but these try his soul and refine it. The precipitate hastiness of the earlier years gives way to calm deliberativeness, and the feverish irritability of youth is replaced by the cool strength of forbearance. In working with human nature a man gets something of the patience of a mother. He is not daunted by a score of failures. He does not surrender to apparent defeat. If doing a thing nineteen times is not sufficient, he is willing to do it the twentieth time.

The grace of humility is watered and unfolded by the shepherd's toil. The minister as preacher is tempted to be conceited. If his sermons are extraordinary, his name is often in the papers. A minister as shepherd has no such temptations. The crowds do not applaud him. His labors do not make good newspaper copy. The pulpiteer is not often made conscious of his failure. Rather, there is always room to hope that someone in the congregation is permanently helped. But the shepherd, working with individuals, faces failure again and again. As a guide he is rejected, his counsel is despised. As a physician he is baffled, the diseases of the soul will not yield. As a savior he is defeated, he cannot bring back a sheep that is lost. There is always a joy in his heart over what he achieves, but there is also always a heaviness because of what he fails to do. "Sorrowing, yet always rejoicing"—this is a fit description of a shepherd's life. He always is being thrown back on God. While some men dream of a speedy ending of evils, and other men trust jauntily to experiments in legislation, he knows the power of sin and realizes that there is no help for the world this side of God. His experience in fighting evil face to face brings him into the dust. Moreover, his work is never done. The preacher can preach his sermon and feel that the task is ended. He can compute the number of discourses that are expected of him in a year and can tell when that number has been written. To a shepherd's work there is no limit. After he has done a thousand things, he can think of a thousand other things still to do. After he has done his best, he feels like confessing himself an unprofitable servant. The shepherd's work is never done.

The mystery of iniquity becomes more and more mysterious to one who works to rescue men from their sins, and a deepening realization of its immeasurable power throws the shepherd back on God in Christ. Faith takes a deepening meaning. He understands as few men do that it is necessary to walk by faith. He learns also why Paul calls hope a helmet, for he knows that without hope he cannot hold his head up in the battle. He comes to know, as few men know, the length and breadth and height and depth of Christian love. He reads, as few men know how to read, Paul's immortal words: "Love suffereth long and is kind; love beareth all things, believeth all

things, hopeth all things, endureth all things."
There are many things which a faithful shepherd
must endure, and when crucified he prays with
Jesus: "Father, forgive them, for they know not
what they do." The faithful shepherd comes to
know the fellowship of Christ's sufferings,
becoming conformable to his death.

One may be a student and a scholar and write
ponderous books of wisdom, and never once
know the meaning of Gethsemane. One may
work glowing ideas into golden speech, and thrill
men's hearts with a tongue which has the wiz-
ardry of genius, and never understand the significance of the cross. But when one becomes a
shepherd and gives his life to shepherding men,
he begins at once to be baptized with the bap-
tism that Jesus was baptized with and to drink
the cup from which Jesus drank. It is not until
one comes out of the library and gets down beside someone who has fallen and is bleeding and
half-dead that one becomes a man of sorrows and
acquainted with grief. If to be Christlike is the
greatest of all privileges, then that privilege belongs preeminently to the shepherd.

It is a reward that is offered to all shepherds,
no matter how large or how small may be their
flock. There is no church in any part of the world
so small or so obscure that it does not furnish
room for the growing of a shepherd-saint. John
Fletcher was pastor for twenty-five years in the
little village of Madeley, and he grew there into

a saint whose name will be fragrant forever. The brilliant Oxford scholar John Keble was for thirty years the pastor of the little village of Hursley, and in that quiet country town he grew to be so much like Jesus that many men declared him to be the saintliest man they had ever known.

When God distributes his rewards he does not ask a minister concerning the size of his church, but simply inquires about the spirit with which he has done his work. To every man who shepherds Christ's sheep is the privilege granted of growing into the likeness of the perfect Shepherd. Large parishes spoil some men, but small parishes spoil others. High positions are dangerous, and so also are positions which are humble. A prominent church may make the minister conceited, but an obscure church may do the same thing. A man in a humble church may become very conscious of the sacrifice he is making and talk about it often. Those who are very conscious of their sacrifice, and voluble about it, are not saints after the fashion of the Lord. There are men in high places who are vain, envious and discontented; and there are men in low places in the same unhappy frame of mind. Wretched is the minister who is sour in spirit because his dream of advancement has not been fulfilled and whose life is a long-drawn repining because he is not allowed to become the shepherd of a larger and finer flock.

It is a consolation for all ministers great or small

that no matter where one may find himself, or how difficult or obscure his field, the way is open to follow in the footsteps of the Good Shepherd and to win at last the crown of glory. It was a faithful village pastor who wrote these words:

> Do the work that's nearest,
>   Tho' it's dull at whiles,
> Helping when we meet them
>   Lame dogs over stiles;
> See in every hedgerow
>   Marks of angel's feet,
> Epics in each pebble
>   Underneath our feet.

We have come at last to the crowning reward: everlasting fellowship with Jesus Christ and unending participation in his glory. Whatever the glory of the Chief Shepherd is, we who are under-shepherds are, if faithful, to share in it. His prayer was and is, "I desire that where I am there they may be also, that they may behold my glory." What that glory is we know not now, but we shall know hereafter. Paul calls it a "crown of righteousness." Peter calls it a "crown of glory." Jesus calls it a "joy." The idea of sharing the life of Jesus Christ himself was the one which sustained Paul in all his tribulations. In the Roman prison he kept repeating to himself phrases such as these: "If we died with him, we shall also live with him: if we endure, we shall also reign with him." This expectation was foundationed on the words of Jesus himself. To a company of drooping and doleful shepherds he said on the night of his betrayal: "I go to prepare a place for you; and if I go and prepare a place for you, I will come again and receive you unto myself, that where I am there you may be also."

John, exiled on the Isle of Patmos, looking out upon a storm-swept world, the scattered Christian congregations burning like candles in the gale, is not daunted by the existing tragedy and disaster, but hears, above the crash and thunder of the tempest, a divine voice saying: "He that overcometh, I will give to him to sit down with me in my throne, as I also overcame and sat down with my Father in his throne."